The Truth

Vol. 2

The Truth

Charles Makepeace

Tampa, Florida

The content associated with this book is the sole work and responsibility of the author. Gatekeeper Press had no involvement in the generation of this content.

The Truth Volume 2

Published by Gatekeeper Press
7853 Gunn Hwy., Suite 209
Tampa, FL 33626
www.GatekeeperPress.com

Copyright © 2024 by Charles Makepeace
All rights reserved. Neither this book, nor any parts within it may be sold or reproduced in any form or by any electronic or mechanical means, including information storage and retrieval systems, without permission in writing from the author. The only exception is by a reviewer, who may quote short excerpts in a review.

Copyright for the image: iStockphoto.com/Smileus

Library of Congress Control Number: 2024938746

ISBN (paperback): 9781662946875
eISBN: 9781662946882

Table of Contents

Introduction	1
Chapter 1 **EYEWITNESS**	5
Chapter 2 **MIND, BODY, SPIRIT**	19
Chapter 3 **A GOOD FATHER**	29
Chapter 4 **LIGHT SWITCH**	47
Chapter 5 **CIVILIZED SOCIETY**	57
Chapter 6 **ISOLATION**	67
Chapter 7 **ABSOLUTELY**	75
Chapter 8 **ONE, THEN TWO, THEN THREE**	83
Chapter 9 **K.I.S.S. SYSTEM**	91
Chapter 10 **FINALLY**	103

Introduction

Have you ever sat down and really thought about what your spiritual beliefs are? We might say we believe and trust in God, but how much do we really believe, and how often do we turn to him for help? Do we even know God? These questions can only be answered by the individual asking themselves.

To help us determine our level of belief, we should first recognize what we pay attention to. Whatever we put time and effort into is what we consider to be of value. If we don't value something, we don't pay any attention at all to it. On the other hand, if we esteem something as valuable, we pay attention to it, and we give it our time and affection. So many marriages fail because one of the spouses says they never felt wanted or loved. We might say we love and cherish something, but we all know actions speak so much louder than words. Personally, I would rather someone never say they love me, so long as I can see it in their actions.

Again, whatever we label as valuable is what we will devote our time and attention to. We all have enough superficial friends for whom we put on a good show, yet we are really blessed if we have one true friend around whom we can be exactly who God intended us to be.

We put on such a good dog-and-pony show throughout our lives, but are we pulling the proverbial wool over our own eyes as well? We are all such good actors. When we first meet someone, we are on our best behavior, and we pay attention to what we say and how we say it so as not to offend or make ourselves look like fools. This changes after we get to know the other, and we feel comfortable letting our true selves out in the open. We stop paying attention to what we say or how we act, because we've gotten tired of trying to impress, and our true self is on full display.

Is our relationship with God just one more show we put on? I have no doubt that many people believe in God, but the question is, how can we know? The depth of any relationship is based on many facets, but one of the main components is trust. How do we know we can trust God? Is our relationship with God just on Sunday mornings for an hour and change, and then we pack him away? Do we include God in our decision making? Do we let God have the first say—or any say at all—in how we manage our lives? I'm not just talking about if we follow the "rules" of religion, such as tithing 10 percent, not eating meat on Fridays, fasting every now and then, and so on. I'm talking about if we know God as well as he knows us. The question of what level of maturity we feel we're at in our spiritual journey is one that can only be answered by ourselves, and if we do not answer it with truth and sincerity, then we're only hurting ourselves. I don't consider myself any better or worse than anyone else on this planet, but I do know I have a good relationship with our Creator, and I try to give him the respect a child would give to his father, because to me this is exactly what faith is all about: a father-child relationship.

We have to recognize that we are all on the level of maturity that we are on, spiritually, mentally, and physically. There's no shame being on any level where we may find ourselves. God loves us with a love we cannot understand until we experience it. The more time and attention we devote to our Creator, the more valuable we will realize this time is. When we do, our relationship with God won't be as forced and superficial as when we meet new people. I'm not saying we need to shave our heads like monks and live in complete silence, with only God on our minds; rather, I'm saying we would be wise to include God in our lives as we would an immediate family member.

We know we can trust God because we've probably all been in a situation in which we had no choice but to trust him, and he came through for us with shining colors. We know we believe in God because we've developed our relationship into what it is. We spend time with him. We share our thoughts and concerns with him. We give him the respect he deserves as our Creator and God, and we treat him as we would a revered parent. When we get to the level of spiritual maturity where we can be ourselves around our Creator, that's when we know what we believe. We have dropped all the masks and acting and have spent enough time with our God to feel comfortable enough to just be ourselves. He has seen us in the good, the bad, and the downright ugly, just a father and child journeying together through time, until we come together in eternity.

May God richly bless you and yours.

Chapter 1
EYEWITNESS

"For we cannot but speak of what we have seen and heard." (Acts 4:20 ESV)

Years ago, when I was younger and new to the faith, I knew about as much of it as a newborn babe. And in hindsight, that is exactly what I was. In my mind, however, I was the next big prophet coming straight out of the desert to save the people from their many, many sins. I was so happy to know that I was forgiven and on my way to spending eternity with our Creator that I couldn't wait to tell everyone else about it. I wanted everyone to know the same offer was available to them as well. Well, now that I'm quite a bit older and have experienced life in all its "awesomeness," I see that not only was I extremely naïve, but I was also quite an oddball and hard to be around. Instead of coming across as a well-educated Bible scholar who knew everything about everything in the Bible, I just came across as weird.

One of the earlier churches I attended would send out teams of people to canvas neighborhoods, and we would preach the Gospel to whoever would listen. I never really felt comfortable doing this, but being young and naïve, I was under the impression it was my duty as a Christian, so along I went. I never spoke up about my discomfort, and truth be told, I wouldn't have known what to say anyway, so I just went along for the ride. I still see people doing this from time to time. I even get a knock on the door every so often from the Jehovah's Witnesses wanting me to attend their church. During witnessing, we would stay out for the allotted time frame, most of the time just annoying people while we knocked on their doors. I always thought this was just a waste of time, but again, I felt duty bound. After all, God had saved and forgiven me, so I felt it was my duty to let other people know all about him too. Well, after living a little and experiencing life with our Creator, I realized it most certainly is my duty, just not in the way I was going about it.

The more time I spend in this world, the more I see what's what. I see the cycles of life. I've seen people being born, I've seen people dying, and I know people who have died. I've noticed the world and its cycles. It comes to life in the spring, thrives throughout the summer, then grows old in the fall, and dies in the winter. I've been around all kinds of animals, some pretty cool, some I don't care to be within a hundred feet of, and everything in between. I've got a million stories of the millions of experiences I've had: some were magical, some not so much. I've been through the whole range of emotions we share as human beings. I know what it means to hurt and why we cry. I know what it means to have a deep belly laugh, when it feels so good to laugh, we can feel it deep down. Sorrow, horror, fear, love, hate, lust, greed, envy, pride—I've experienced the whole range. I can remember the absolute best day of my life, when my first son was born. I can remember the absolute worst days of my life, when it seemed I was trapped in a downward spiral and couldn't escape. I've experienced life. Just plain life. Emotions and feelings are a wonderful gift, and I believe I've been through them all. The older we get, and the more we live this life, the more emotions we'll experience, and eventually be through the list in our own lives.

We've all got a story to tell. Mostly, that's all our conversations are anyway, right? When we're sitting at lunch with our co-workers, when we're at the dinner table with our family, when we're listening to a preacher explain the Bible, or when we're watching a movie. We all love a good movie, right? Movies are just an interesting story about a character and all their exploits. Even the news is just people telling us the latest story of what's been going on in the world. When we boil it all down, either we're telling a story or we're listening to one. I would venture to say that 99 percent of what comes out of our mouths is in some way associated with telling a story. Hey, friend, how was your weekend? Oh, let me tell you what happened. Hey, so-and-so, how are you? Well, this happened, that happened, but other than that, I guess I'm okay. It's all about stories. If we've been born into this world, we have a story.

When we're down and we feel empty and alone, it can be comforting to know that someone understands what we're feeling and can sympathize with us, doesn't it? You bet it does. When we feel beat down, the first thing we think is that no one understands, that we're in this alone, and that there's no way out. But if someone else has experienced what we're going through and they came out okay, then there must be hope for me. Hope is a beautiful thing. Hope, in my opinion, ranks way up there at the top of the spectrum of emotions we experience.

There's no better feeling than knowing there's something to look forward to. I may not have what I need right now, but I know it's on the way. I'm crying my eyes out, but I know better days are coming. It's pouring rain outside, but I know the sun is still in the sky, it's just covered with a bunch of clouds right now, it'll be back soon. Life is all about perspective, and we can all use a nudge in the right direction from time to time, like when we've gotten so worn out that we start to lose hope. Just like hope can be one the best feelings, one of the worst feelings is feeling like there is no hope.

God is trying to show us through our experiences that there is never a reason to lose hope. Hope is the fuel that drives our emotions in a positive direction. When there is something to look forward to, it just adds a zest to life and living that just feels good. "For no matter how many promises God has made, they are "Yes" in Christ. And so, through him the "Amen" is spoken by us to the glory of God" (2 Corinthians 1:20 NIV). All of God's Old Testament promises are fulfilled in Jesus. Christ is the "Yes" to every one of them. God has given us new promises and made a new agreement with us. "For this is the covenant that I will make with the house of Israel after those days, declares the Lord: I will put my laws into their minds, and write them on their hearts, and I will be their God, and they shall be my people. And they shall not teach, each one his neighbor and each one his brother, saying, 'Know the Lord' for they shall all know me, from the least of them to the greatest. For I will be merciful towards their iniquities, and I will remember their sins no more" (Hebrews 8:10-12 NIV).

Here we find God offering us a new agreement, with new promises. What could have seemed to us impossible has been made possible. God has made life foolproof for us, and promised to take care of everything that pertains to us, and that is more than enough reason for us to have hope. The more time we spend with our Creator, the more we can see these promises in action. Yet, it takes time, effort and attention for this to manifest in our lives. What we once perceived as impossible, in time will be perceived as the mode of operation.

Perspective is how we interpret what we see. Two people could read the exact same thing and yet have two different opinions on what they've read. When we experience something, we use our brains to categorize what we've seen. How developed our perspective is and what our views are on life and living are will determine how we categorize our experience. For example, say it's cloudy outside. One person concludes that it's getting ready to rain and the weather will be miserable all day. Another person views it as good news, because they work outside and will be working in the shade instead of a bright hot sun beating down on them. These two people are both looking at the same situation with two different views of it and two different perspectives.

We develop perspective throughout our lives and through our experiences. Just like with emotions, there is a wide spectrum of perspectives that can develop in our human psyche. Perspective can cover a wide range, from "Life is being born just so we can die," to "Everything in life is so full of excitement and wonder, and it's just awesome." We all live somewhere along this spectrum of perspective. How do we see life? That choice is solely upon the one life was given to us. Our experiences have determined our perspective. We can choose how we see this life, and what we choose to see determines the experiences we will have. I have been everywhere on that spectrum, from "Why try, since everything is going terribly anyway?" to "I can't wait to see what's next, and life is great." In fact, I'd venture to say that we've all been in between those two poles.

Just like we've all got a story, so all our stories range from magic to tragic. We've experienced some of the best this life has to offer, and we have experienced the worst this life has to offer. The one thing I've come to learn is how to manage it. If we allow it, our perspectives can change with the blowing wind. It may be bright and sunny in the morning and cloudy and raining in the afternoon, but if I know how to manage my perspective, I'm not swayed either way. I'm not too high when it's good, and I'm not too low when it's bad. I've learned to be content and at peace with both.

I try to accept what's what as it is, not as I would want it. There are a lot of bad things going on in this world today, and it can drain us dry if we allow it. Which side of the perspective spectrum we live on will determine how well we live out this existence. Are we going to just give up and stop trying because everything's going to crap anyway, or are we going to roll up our sleeves and get to work? Everything that Jesus said was going to happen is happening now, and he is on the way back to take us with him to eternity. "You will hear of wars and rumors of wars but, see to it that you are not alarmed. Such things must happen, but the end is still to come. Nation will rise against nation, and kingdom against kingdom. There will be famines and earthquakes in various places. All these are the beginning of birth pains" (Matthew 24:6-8 NIV).

In my haste to be the next mega-church world-renowned pastor, I failed to realize that I didn't know anything. Of course, I went to church and put on quite the show, and I even went a step further to get more checks on my checklist by attending Sunday school. Yes, sir, extra credit for this guy! Now that I'm older, and certainly wiser, all I can say is "Wow." I couldn't have been more fake in those years. I knew nothing about anything, and acted like I was fourth in the lineup of the trinity. It's God, Jesus, the Holy Spirit, and then me—yours truly. I really was that bad. Sure, I knew the stories in the Bible, and even somewhat where to find them. Yet that's where my story ended. There was no relationship being built, no growth, just me throwing around relevant verses to whatever conversation we were having at the time. God, through his lovingkindness, brought me through experiences where I could see the superfluous repetition of my behavior. When it finally dawned on me to listen to the real God and what he was trying to convey to me, I realized God was talking to me about what he was talking about at that time in my life. I had confused it with God talking to me to tell everyone else, when all the while he was giving me the info just for me. Slowly, I began to realize it, and apply it to my own life, which rearranged my shallow perspective of life. I began to understand what we were trying to teach others, and the hope that we were offering in accepting Jesus. My understanding of hope went from "I accepted Jesus as my savior and am on my way to spending eternity with him." to "I accepted Jesus as my savior, I am now an adopted child of the most high God, and I am blessed to be taught how to experience this existence to its fullest, as I look forward to living forever in peace and harmony with my Father in Heaven."

The hope that was once forced and insincere had become real and tangible. God took my superficial perspective and brought me through multiple life experiences that showed to me that God keeps his promises and does what he says he will. The hope that has been developed in me now is this: "when" God shows up for me, not will he. I now see life and living in a whole different light than before, and it has become my hope that you will as well. Life is better spent with the one who created it, and he has given us the greenlight to do just that. Ask yourself where you think you rank on the hope scale. Do you know that you know God does what he says he will, and you live life accordingly? Are you being taught? Are you open to being taught? We are the only ones who can answer those questions for ourselves, but if we are living life less than I know God as the loving Father he claims to be, we are living way below our potential.

Looking back, I'm glad I'm not that guy anymore. Then God came along—the real one, not me in sandals and a sheet—and let me tell you, it's been quite the journey. I had a story before God came along, but now I can relate to the stories I preached for years and years. I would go around quoting verse after verse with no real power behind them. I was just quoting what I read, but I hadn't lived them. When I lived those verses, that's when they became real to me and gave me a story to tell. I became a witness, if you will. Then I saw with a different perspective all those trips we took to people who just wanted us to shut up and go away. All we did for them was quote what we had read and been programmed to say. We had a script we would read, but when you broke it down, it was all just an invitation to come to church. We constantly referred to it as witnessing for Christ, when in reality, how could we be a witness to something if we weren't there and never experienced it?

I never really thought for myself back then; I just went with the church crowd and did what they did, acted like they acted, and tried to keep a low profile. Talk about herd mentality. I went to church because that's what "good" people did. I give all the credit to God for intervening in my life, because if it weren't for him, I would still be in some church, going through the same routines, never grasping why we go there in the first place. Throughout the years of my life, God gradually opened my eyes to the truth and what the truth is. The truth of our whole existence can be summed up by saying that God created us for the purpose of having a relationship with us. God is our Father, and we are his children. That's it. Nothing more, nothing less. Witnessing for Christ is all well and good, but if it's taken out of context, which it far too often is, it could potentially do more harm than good.

I mentioned that I was young and naïve, and that's something we've all had the pleasure of being. We all start out as know-nothing babies, and we grow into what we are now. We add pages to our individual stories every day. We experience life, and we develop perspectives. God is God. He is our Creator, and we were created after his design, so he knows everything about us. We, on the other hand, start out as infants, know nothing, need to be taught. Everything pertaining to our understanding is something we've been taught and that we've learned. That's just the way it works. Once we are taught something, then we can understand and know what we've been taught. What we've been taught then becomes part of us. Our brains aren't very good at unlearning something, but they excel at gathering new information. We can forget stuff if we don't deem it important, but we can't just hit a delete button and move stuff to our trash bins. Once we experience something, it becomes a learned thing.

Throughout our lives, God is trying to get us to understand the truth. He wants us to know the truth about him, the truth about ourselves, the whole truth and nothing but the truth about everything pertaining to our existence. God is a good Father. His very being is love. We have to be taught, and God is the best teacher. We get so ahead of ourselves in our search for understanding, and we can so easily be led astray. Most of us don't even realize how much we need God's guidance in our lives. Yes, it's a wonderful thing to realize God has forgiven us and welcomed us to the family, but when we take that out of context and think that's all there is to our education, then we've missed the point. That's just the first step, not the last step of the journey. Yes, we are called to be witnesses for Christ, but we have to understand what that means first. It's great to share our newfound family, but we need to share what we know, not what we're guessing. What we know at that present moment of our lives, when we first accept Christ, is an overwhelming sense of love and peace, which it is. But that's all we know of it so far.

The mysteries of heaven and earth aren't automatically unlocked, and no one is given understanding about everything all at once. If that was your experience, then I need to talk to the manager, because my experience was quite the opposite, and I'm a little miffed to say the least. The truth is that we have each started a lifelong journey of understanding. The only difference between then and now is that we've chosen to follow Christ as he teaches us. We've given God permission to be present in our lives, to be our Father as well our Creator.

It truly is a blessing when we first accept God as our God, and if that's something any of us haven't done, I suggest we do so now. But we can't allow ourselves to fall in the pitfall of thinking that's the final step. I fell headfirst into that trap, and I can say in all sincerity that I was wrong. For years I was not even close to the truth, and I've seen too many people fall into the same trap. They allow God into their lives, they believe they are "saved" as we like to put it, and they think they know everything about spirituality. Even now, when I try to talk to someone, I can usually tell exactly where they are in their walk with God. How? Because when I was at that level, I did the exact same thing. I'm not better or worse than anyone, I'm just where I'm at.

Just like how we label time, we could probably label people as well. We might say that BC stands for "before Christ," and AD stands for "After Death." BC means before Christ entered my life. AD means after I died and Christ took over. And when I say "died," that's just church jargon for when I stopped relying on my own wisdom and started accepting the truth for what it is, not the way I'd like it to be. This is where we can do more harm than good when it comes to witnessing for Christ. If we don't know, it's okay to admit we don't know. It does more harm to people when we guess at the truth, and twist it around so that it looks like we know what we're talking about. But if we haven't got to that point in our education, how can we relate it to anyone? We might pretend to others, but God knows where we are in our maturity level. I could be one hundred years old but have the spiritual fortitude of a five-year-old. I don't know everything about the truth, but God does. God teaches us what we need to know, and he teaches us when we need it. It's up to us how long it takes for us to learn. The more time we spend with God, the more understanding we can learn. And the more we learn, the more pages are added to our story, our witness.

I planted a garden once, a really big one. I had a little bit of everything, and once everything was planted, all I could do was sit back and watch. I would go out every morning before the sun came up and water it from one end to the other. I used the same method, the same dirt, the same water, the same everything for all the plants. I had melons on one end, tomatoes on another with their little cages to grow around, cucumbers, some squash, and even some zucchini. Time went by, and I started to notice little seedlings popping up. As excited as I was, I noticed that while some of the plants progressed, some weren't doing anything at all. How could that be? I did the exact same thing with all of them. Same dirt, same methods, same everything. I put my research in and cared for each plant like each one should have been cared for. Yet while one would grow well, another, with the exact same conditions, seemed to struggle. Why? To this day, I have no clue. The older I've gotten, the more I see what that means. Just like my garden, our world has so many different people, on so many different levels of understanding, that all we can do is care for them all. When it comes to what grows and what doesn't, that's not for us to decide. The growth belongs to God

Our lives develop as we experience them. Our perspectives will change when God shows us things in a different light. Our hope will grow from *will this happen* to *when this happens* in our lives. God loves us and wants nothing less than the best for each of us, and this comes with growing and maturing into the beings we were created to be. All of God's promises are "Yes," but with that yes comes a responsibility on our part of being mature enough to understand what we're receiving. God will not forgive us if we refuse to forgive others. God will not bless us if we are being a curse to others, in whatever scenario. God uses our experiences to shape and mold us into mature, well-established children, which in turn gives us our personal story of redemption. The Bible, too, is just a book with its own stories until we live those stories. When we do, they become real to us. God knows each one of us. We think we know what we need, but God knows what we need and when we need it. God is God. Let's all move to the AD label of life. Let God teach us who God is. Let God teach us the truth, and stop writing our own fictional book. God will write us a new story about life and living, if we allow him to. Then when we are a witness for Christ, it will come from our lived experience.

That's what being a witness is: telling a story about what happened. When I was broke as a joke, God gave me money to pay my bills with. When I was sick lying in a hospital bed, God healed me. When I was so broken that I couldn't take it anymore, God showed up and gave me love. All these and much more are the stories we all have to share. We're not going house-to-house inviting people to church; all we're doing is sharing a story of what happened and who made it happen. In turn, when God gives us more of our story, the further up the perspective ladder we can go. My perspective has drastically improved, because I've seen—not read in a book, but seen with my own two eyes and experienced with all my senses—that God is God and that he does what he says he will do. How will he do it? No clue. I just know he will. When things are pitch-black and all seems lost, I know I'm just getting closer to what God has in store for my next chapter. It's been quite the story so far. No matter where we find ourselves, always know, and cling to this, that if God seems like he's nowhere to be found, that's because he's got you on his back and he's carrying you till you can find the strength to walk for yourself. Be patient, be honest, and be the change you want to see in everyone else. Above all, be blessed as we walk with God and in his love.

God bless you and yours.

Chapter 2
MIND, BODY, SPIRIT

After a day's work, I have a routine of coming home, resting for a while, catching my breath, then cleaning myself up before I make myself dinner and relax for the evening. Last night, when I was getting out of the shower and passing in front of the mirror behind my sink, I thought, "What an impressive piece of machinery." No, I was not impressed with the sight of my body. There's nothing impressive about my physique at all. I'm not talking about my ripped abs (which are cleverly hidden behind my round belly). I'm talking about the overall mechanics. The whole makeup. The brain, the nervous system, the heart, the stomach, the genitals—all of it is such an impressive thing. Everything works together to support the whole being and makes it function as it does. The heart pumps the life-giving blood, which flows through the body to all the other organs, which all have their individual functions. The body is just awesome.

Not only is the body an impressive, well-put-together, and well-organized piece of hardware, but it also comes with its own failsafe programs preinstalled. Our bodies will automatically tell us what they need. We know when we need to eat to recharge our energy levels, we know when we need to drink, and we know when it's time to get rid of the waste. Our bodies just do what they do, and as long as we provide them with what they are calling for, they will be just fine. We have this wonderful thing called pain, which our nervous system provides us with, to let us know when something is causing our bodies harm or damage. When something happens that is detrimental to our bodily functions, we instantly know because of those pain signals that our system puts out. The function of our bodies is just amazing to me. What an awesome machine.

Our physical bodies aside, exploring the rest of our makeup is a little bit trickier. We all know we have emotions, but how to define them is much trickier. When I searched the internet for a definition of emotions, it said, "There is currently no scientific consensus on a definition." Wow! We know what the emotions are, but we just can't explain them.

Emotions, to me, are how the mind expresses the information it has received. When we smile, that means something is pleasing and inviting to us. When we frown or cry, that usually means something is displeasing and uninviting to us. We understand the range of emotions we all have, and we know the triggers that are involved in releasing them. We've concluded what causes what, so we can now deduce that emotions are just the way the brain expresses its information through the body's functions. The body tells the brain something is pleasing, the mind tells the body to smile, and so we smile.

Emotions are the way we express what we are experiencing. There's a wide range of emotions, but when we boil it all down, we have positive emotions and negative emotions. We constantly experience both sides of the spectrum. Just like many of our physical bodily functions, our emotions are usually involuntary.

Whatever emotions we are experiencing, our minds will express through our bodies the appropriate physical response. Through our experiences, we know what those responses mean. Feeling sad is expressed through frowning or crying; feeling happy through smiling or excitement; feeling anger through turning red, scrunching our face, and so on. For the most part, we've lived with ourselves long enough to know what triggers our emotional responses. The older we get, the better we get either at controlling or hiding our emotions.

The third and certainly most important aspect of our makeup is our spirit. The spirit is the glue that holds everything together. The Bible teaches us that the human spirit is the very breath of God, our Creator. Then the Lord God formed a man from the dust of the ground and breathed into his nostrils the breath of life, and the man became a living being" (Genesis 2:7 KJV). Our spirit is the very thing that lets us know that we are alive. It allows us the ability to think, feel, and experience emotions. I'm not even going to attempt to explain our spirit other than what the Bible says it is: the very breath of God. God has given our physical bodies the ability to be alive and be aware of our existence. We can't comprehend how it happens; we just know it does. Unlike our emotions, which are expressed through our bodily gestures, our spirits cannot be seen or felt, and yet we know they are there. How do we know? Because we're alive, and as long as we're living, our spirit provides the ability to use our bodies and emotions to express the experiences we have. In essence, the spirit is the fuel that allows us to live. Without the spirit, there is no life.

We are a very well put together piece of hardware. I for one am quite impressed. Just like every piece of hardware and equipment, the better it is maintained, the better its performance. I love watching football, and sports in general, and I would have to say those players are in top form. They have worked their bodies into optimal shape to perform at a high level of competition. We spend a lot of time and energy on keeping our bodies in optimal working order. Some of us only eat the healthiest of foods, some only eat vegetables and fruits. Some of us live in gyms, working out. The majority of us understand the importance of keeping our bodies functioning at their highest levels, and push our bodies to attain maximum efficiency. We've come to learn that the better we feel, the better we act. In essence, our emotions are expressing the health of our bodies through positive emotions.

We understand the body, and to some extent, we can understand the emotional responses we express, but what about the spirit? Even if we've come to understand all about the mind and body, we often don't give much thought to our spirit. Why is this? Is it because we can't see or feel our spirit, and we downgrade its importance? Perhaps. Yet our spirit is the most vital part of us. As we've learned, our spirit is the fuel that provides us life. If our spirit is damaged and broken, we can't live life to its optimal level. Sure, we can still perform, but it won't be at the quality we could have if our spirit was healthy and thriving.

Unlike our bodies and emotions, we can't see our spirit. Our spirit could be so broken that we live life at half the capacity we could be living at and not even be aware of it. For years, I carried around so much anger and hate and never knew why. I never learned about my spirit, because I was never taught. I always thought this was just the way life was, and to some extent, that's true. It was the way it is, but it's not the way it has to be. I never gave any thought to my spirit, until God encouraged me to learn about my total makeup, not just my mind and body. When I honestly started to pay attention to what I was learning in church, God opened my eyes to a whole new level of understanding. We know we're a three-part being, mind, body, and spirit. The truth is they are all equally important and function as one unit to make the whole being of who we are. We can see and feel the first two aspects of our being, but the third and most important, is hidden deep within us all. We have experienced a lot of pain and hurt throughout our life, some of us to the point of seemingly irreparable damage. I intentionally used the word *we*, because this experience is universal. We all experience life and all the emotions associated with it, and unfortunately, hurt and pain are included in this list.

We put so much effort and energy into maintaining our bodies, but we should at the very least be aware of our spirit and its health. Even if we choose to not address the issues we may or may not have, let's at least be open to the fact that our spiritual health could be enhanced if we allow it. We've all experienced trauma in whatever form it may have taken in our respective lives, and it has played a part in who we have become. Whatever experience it may have been, we've developed ways of how we cope with it. Our natural response is to forget about it. We bury it so deep in our psyche and never talk about it. The issue with this is the trauma never heals. Think of it as a cut on the body. If we cut ourselves, we immediately do what we must do to stop the bleeding. Action was taken to correct the issue. If nothing was done and we never addressed the bleeding, we would eventually bleed out. Same concept with our spirits. If we never address the issue that caused our spirits damage, the damage continues to fester and will mutate into something worse than what it was. The truth of the matter is, if we haven't used the tools God has given us to deal with trauma, then it will remain traumatic years after the actual event, and in essence it will have molded you into who you are. We will be maturing into forgiving, understanding people, because we have learned how to address the traumatic events of our lives in the proper way. Or, we will be stuck in neutral, never progressing, because we have unresolved issues in our spiritual health that we never addressed.

Our mental health is vital to our well-being. Everything in our being works in harmony with the other. Our bodies express what our emotional state is. Our emotional state is reflected in how we file what we've experienced, and our spirit is the hub of it all. Everything works together as one: whatever we experience is turned into emotions, which in turn is expressed through our body; it also goes straight to our spirit and becomes who we are. If our spirit is alive and healthy, it will show through our emotions and how we relate to life. If our spirit is damaged and broke, that will affect how we relate to life too. Whether the state of our spirit is positive or negative, it will come out in our lives either way. There are so many drugs available today that attend to so many different aspects of our mental state. And yet they only mask the underlying issues; they don't resolve the problem; they only help with the problem. That's not really healthy. I can put on bandage upon bandage, but if I never stop the source of the bleeding, I'm not fixing anything. In the end, the bandages will have only prolonged my life until I died without providing any real solution.

We've all been through the gamut of emotions and experienced life with ups, downs, and everything in between. We've all been through the whole range of emotions we all share as human beings. We understand how and why our bodies work, we understand how and why our emotions are what they are, but we've only scratched the surface on our spirituality and its health. For whatever reason, our society has labeled mental health and spiritual health as weak and inferior (though we do seem to be getting more mature about it). Why? Our bodies work as a whole, and all of those areas make up who and what we are, so it would be only logical to take care of our whole being instead of just a few of the moving parts, right? In my opinion, the devil knows how important the spiritual area of our existence is, and he has made every attempt to minimize its importance. If the devil can keep us focused on our bodies and mental health, then he can keep the main focus a secondary afterthought. Every other commercial on TV is a new drug designed for whatever may ail our body. Every so often we may see an advertisement about checking your mental health, but there is nothing about anything that pertains to understanding our spiritual health. We are all damaged in our psyche and in our spirit, and this in turn leads us to live a less-than-optimal life. Once we know what is causing us the pain and hurt that damages our spirit, we need to understand the why, as well as what we can do about it.

It's time we paid attention to all aspects of our being, not just what we can see and feel. Truthfully, it's what we can't see and feel that determines the quality of our lives. When our mental state is good, it shows in our emotions. We smile, we laugh, we joke. When our mental state is not so good, that shows as well. We frown, or we become stoic, hiding our emotion. It's time we get to the root of our issues, so we can develop real solutions to our real problems. How? If our spirits are the breath of God, then he would know exactly what's been damaged and not in optimal working order. God is the answer. God knows exactly how to mend and repair what's not working in us, and the best part is that he knows why.

There are stories after stories about people at their wits' end, close to committing suicide, and the way they choose to do it just doesn't work. The gun jammed. The rope snapped. The pills didn't work. Afterward, they all relate the same experience: they heard a voice tell them there is another way. How beautiful: God came to them and stopped them from doing something permanent to a quite fixable situation. I've been there; we all have. The pain is just too much, and it's been carried around long enough. This has to end. We can't stand another minute of it. Sadly, this experience is because of a broken and damaged spirit. We know we have the pain, because we have it every second of every day. What we don't know is why. This is where God comes into our lives. God knows exactly why and what to do about it. He will most certainly help us come to terms with our spiritual malfunctions, and he will lead us into what needs to be done to restore our spiritual health. There are many reasons why our spirit may be in pain, and they are all legitimate reasons. We just have to humble ourselves before our God and allow him to show us the way back to wholeness and health in all aspects of our lives.

I encourage all who read this to examine yourselves and see if there's still some pain in your spirit. Then come to God with it. No pretenses; just you and your Maker. Tell him about it, how it made you feel, how it hurt you, how angry it made you feel. God is the best listener in existence. God wants to hear from us; he wants to raise us back up to living a quality, healthy, mature life. God loves to see us smile and enjoy life. Every day, not just every now and again. The time has come to pay just as much attention to our spirit and mental health as we do to our physical health. We are a three-part being: mind, body, and spirit, working as one. If one gets damaged, we feel it in all three aspects until the damage is repaired. Let's grow together, working with our Creator as he restores us to optimal health in all three aspects of our being.

May God richly bless you and yours.

Chapter 3

A GOOD FATHER

For as long as I can remember, I've had dogs. I took a break from owning any when I was married, because as any of us know, marriage and raising a family is quite a lot of work. Yet in the past ten or so years, I've gotten back into owning some animals. I do love my dogs. Sometimes they can get on my very last nerve, but when it's all said and done, I love them very much. I enjoy watching them grow from pups to full-grown adults, and I like seeing how they take on my character and personality. When I watch those SPCA ads that show the rescue of poor animals that are neglected or abused, it makes me so angry. Why take on the responsibility of caring for an animal if that's all the love and respect you have for it?

Raising a pet is a lot like raising a child. It's all fun and games until they start getting older and having a voice of their own. We love cuddling with babies, but when our kids hit those teenage years and start rebelling and growing into their own personality—oh man, how fun is that? Yet no matter how rebellious or wild they get, they're still our children, and we still love them no matter what. Why can't animals get the same respect? Most dogs aren't rebellious at all. Sure, some breeds are stubborn and difficult, but with a little training and patience, they grow out of it.

Training a dog is not that difficult. It does require a certain amount of patience and fortitude, but it can be done. What's worked best for me is having a good schedule. When I train my new dogs, I try to keep to a precise schedule. We eat at the same or near the same time every day. When they first wake up, the first thing they do is go outside to relieve themselves. Then they eat, then they can do whatever they want, whether that's going outside or lying around. I do try to always have at least two dogs, so they can have a playmate and not get bored. Then in the late afternoon they eat again. Afterward, they mostly go out and run around in the yard, and then it's bedtime. I've raised enough dogs that I've learned what works and what doesn't, especially when it comes to potty training. It's on me to be diligent and watch them for signs that they're getting ready to use the bathroom in the house, so I can redirect to where they should go. I can't expect my dogs to know what's right and what's not if I never teach them. And that goes for children as well, right? We get mad at our children for misbehaving, when it's on us to give them the proper tools for a given situation. They attempt to do what they think is right, and when it backfires, we get all bent out of shape over it. In the end, it's our failure for not teaching, not theirs for screwing something up.

The more of a routine my animals have, the better they become at it. They know what time they do what they do. The first thing they do when I get them in the morning is run right to the back door. When I let them back in, they run right to their food bowls. When they're done eating, they hang out and do what they do with their free time. When the next feeding comes around, they usually let me know what time it is, because they've gotten so used to their schedule. Same thing when they need something. They'll come and get me, and they know what to do to get my attention. It's funny, because we have been around one another long enough to understand what we're talking about. When they're thirsty, they'll come and get me to follow them to their water dish. When they need the backyard to go to the bathroom or to play, they get me and lead me to the backyard door. With the two I have now, we've developed quite a relationship. I've come to understand them, and they've come to understand me.

Relationships are built and created. When my first son was born, he had no clue who I was. Of course, no babies know anything about anything; that's what makes them so amazing. As their parents, we will mold those children into what they will be, until they experience enough life to become what they've been created for. It takes time though, doesn't it? Years and years of engaging with one another and feeling out what makes the other tick: "Your faults as a son is my failure as a father." Very true indeed. A teacher teaches more by what they do than by what they say. When I hear you say something, I can come up with all sorts of interpretations as to what you meant. However, if I see you do something, there's no need for words. I gathered the information by what I saw you do, and there's no room for guesswork. I saw exactly how it was done, so I can't question it. The more we pay attention to how we experience this existence, we can see more and more of God's love for us. When we witness God keeping his promises, we experience his love. When God rescues us from a bad situation, we experience his love. We can constantly see God as the father he claims to be if we just pay attention, and give credit where credit is due.

    This is a major aspect of relationships. Do we do what we say? Are we true to our word? Doing what we say we will do builds trust, and trust is the cornerstone of any relationship. If I see I can't trust you, it will be hard to build anything else, because I'll never believe you even if you are telling the truth. My dogs run straight to their food bowls when it's feeding time. Why? Because they've done it enough to know that this is the time I give them their food. They don't question it. They don't argue with me. They've been around me long enough to know that this is feeding time, and they've seen it enough to understand what it means. The more time we spend with our God and move through life together, we will begin to see the truth for what it is. The truth being God is love, and he loves us with a love we cannot understand until we experience it, and even then, it takes time for us to accept that as truth. The sooner we can come to terms with a loving God wanting nothing more than to love his creation, the deeper we can go in our relationship with our God. We need to become like my dogs. We need to get to the level of understanding that our God loves us. When we are in need, we need to bring our thoughts and concerns to our God, and he will provide a way to meet our need, no matter what it is. The more we invest in spending time with our God, the faster we will be on our way to a solid understanding of who he is and what he's about, and we will not question if there's going to be dinner tonight, we will run right to our dinner table, patiently awaiting what God has provided for us for that day. All for that fact that we have come to terms with God loving us for who we are.

It will take time and effort to get to the point of understanding that God loves us unconditionally. We can read it over and over in the Bible. Isaiah 54:10. Ephesians 2:8. Jeremiah 31:3. John 3:16. 1 John 3:1. Romans 5:8. We can read what God has said about the situation, but we then have to experience it to fully grasp the concept. God will bring us through experience after experience as he proves to us his nature and what love truly means. The point of the matter is how far are we willing to go. God will be your everything and anything, if you only allow it. The deeper we decide to go will determine the level of understanding we have. I know that I know God is God because I have experienced it time and time again. No matter what level we may find ourselves on, there is always room for growth, and an opportunity for a more profound, deeper knowledge of God. The choice is ours on how deep or shallow we want to be in our relationship with our Creator, but I assure you God has given us every opportunity to learn and mature, the lack of understanding falls completely on our shoulders.

I can only give you what I have, right? It's impossible for me to give you something I don't physically possess. The same goes for our mental and spiritual aspects. I can only do what I know. If all I know is partying like a rock star and living the full bachelor life, then that's what I have to offer. If you like having multiple partners at once, then that's what I can expect from you if I want a relationship with you. It reminds me of that story about the woman and the venomous scorpion. One day, a woman was hiking on a trail in the middle of the desert when she came across one of the rarest, most venomous scorpions known to man. She knew how aggressive they were when approached, yet when she got closer, she noticed it was badly hurt and in desperate need of attention. She took up the scorpion and brought it home. She began to nurse the scorpion back to health, and after some time she noticed it was all well. She leaned in to give a kiss, and the scorpion stung and killed her. She wondered within herself why. Why did this scorpion do that after all she had done for it? An answer came from within, "You knew what this was when you first picked it up."

Have you heard the term "red flag"? That's the term we use to describe a situation when we first meet someone and something feels a bit off, or perhaps we notice something that could be a sign of trouble. With one of my last long-term relationships I had, I knew that I knew I was headed for trouble when it first started. My spirit was so uneasy most of the time, and all I could do was find new and improved ways to ignore it. Let me be the first to tell you, to listen to your spirit. Your emotions and feelings will let you down. Your intellect can be tricked. But your spirit will never steer you wrong. We know exactly when we're getting ready to do something dumb. Our spirit will do everything but jump out and slap us clear in the face to try to get us to listen to its advice. Why don't we just listen? Maybe it's because of pride. Maybe it's because we've waited so long for our desires to be met that when the first thing comes along, we throw all caution and sound advice away just to get what we've been longing for. Whatever the reason, I do know that a certain relationship literally almost killed me. The short version of the story is that I ended up in the hospital for three days, recovering from a bad night of drinking and taking pills that weren't prescribed to me. It wasn't a suicide attempt; I just had a bad reaction between the booze and medicine. All this could have been avoided if I had just heeded the advice my spirit was offering me.

We live life so blind sometimes, it's a wonder any of us survive it. When we were younger, we thought we just had to have that good-looking girl or guy whom we had such a crush on, and if we couldn't get them, we'd just die. Looking back, what would we have done if we did get them? We'd probably have found out that beauty is often just skin deep. We've all done it. We jumped into a relationship because the physical attraction was so strong, and we forgot all about investigating all the other aspects of the person. We all like sex; it's one of the best gifts our Creator gave us. However, the physical side of any relationship is only one of the many facets of a relationship. Our Creator put limits on it just for this reason. It was a gift meant to be experienced only after we've been married, designed just for the couple to enjoy with each other. Yet we've decided to make our own rules and put the cart five miles ahead of the horse. Yes, physical attraction is one building block of forming a relationship, but it shouldn't be put first and foremost. I've been around so many different people, and I used to judge along those same lines. Wow, she's gorgeous, but her personality is hitting zero, and I can't keep her out of the mirror long enough to have a quality conversation. Or sometimes it's that I love hanging out with her, and we have some of the best conversations, and we really get each other, but she could use some help in the make-up department. (Yes, I know that's very shallow. Trust me, I've grown a lot since then.)

Relationships are just separate things coming together. That's it. It's taking a few things and making them one. That's true not just for romantic relationships but also for everything. You have a brief relationship with the fast-food cashier from whom you ordered your food. We have relationships with our co-workers at work. We have relationships with our animals, our kids, our vehicles, and our homes. Relationships are everywhere and with all sorts of things. Therefore, learning what a relationship is and isn't is important to us all. No matter how well-versed we may think we are on the topic, there's always room for growth. Having a non-romantic relationship is fairly cut-and-dried; If we get along, then we hang out; the more we hang out, the more or less we find we have in common, which determines our level of friendship. Perhaps we're friends, but the level of friendship is determined by our compatibility. Do we think like each other? Do we act like each other? Do we trust each other?

Romantic relationships are a bit trickier, right? We give more of ourselves to the other person in the relationship. We bring a different level of openness to the relationship. We can only fake who we are for so long. Eventually, the true self comes to light, and we see exactly what we've signed up for. I see the true you, and you see the true me. Therefore, jumping straight to the physical aspect of the relationship is not such a smart thing. If we get straight to the point and share our most intimate selves, then there's nothing to look forward to. Moreover, we haven't developed the other aspects of the relationship. I could be great at the physical side of relationships but be quite a novice when it comes to all the other aspects. We jump right to the sex and become blind to everything else because the sex was so good. Too often, we jump right to the physical aspect when we start a relationship. The only problem? We're building a roof before we build the house.

The Bible says to guard your heart at all costs (Proverbs 4:23). When we share the most intimate parts of ourselves with another person, we become attached physically. It doesn't matter if the person we just had sex with is a professional sex worker, a one-night stand, or our long-term partner; we will have feelings for that person. It may not seem like it, but it's true. The more we share physically with someone, the more feelings we develop, and the more attached we get. We get adept at burying our feelings just so we can have the pleasure of fulfilling our physical desires, which will eventually turn into a raging fire of lust, where nothing will ever be enough. The deeper we delve into the lust of the flesh, the further we sink into an unhealthy balance of mind, body, and soul. We may be satisfying our physical urges, but our minds and bodies are taking the brunt of the punishment. By denying or suppressing our feelings and emotions, we are not validating that they exist, and feelings and emotions need to be expressed or they will be repurposed into other emotions and feelings such as rage and anger, and then expressed. Either way, emotions need to be expressed. When we lie to ourselves it causes more harm than we know, and causes an unhealthy balance between the three phases of our being.

Therefore, the majority of us, if not all of us, have damaged and broken spirits. The pain may have been self-inflicted by our bad choices, a crush could have crushed us, our parental figures could have let us down, someone we trusted seemingly stabbed us square in the back. Whatever it was, our hearts have been broken, and I for one think that's a real physical condition. We've been hurt so badly by those we thought we loved that it shook us to our very souls. When it was my turn to experience a broken heart, it literally felt like my heart stopped beating and fell into my stomach. Just like sex ranks as the best physical pleasure, a broken heart must rank as the worst.

To say we've all been hurt is the understatement of the century. We have. All of us. When we were young, we had no clue what a relationship was. Men think, if I could just get her in bed and have her on my arm worshiping my every move, then all will be well. Women develop these fantasies in which the handsome prince comes along and sweeps them off their feet and makes them his queen. All these and many more are just young fantasies, thought up by young and immature minds. We did, however, do a lot of dating with a lot of people, and came into those relationships with our vain imaginations as to how they should go in full swing. We started relationships based on our ideals and couldn't seem to understand why they're not going according to our imaginary thoughts. Then we get discouraged as we see that others have a mind of their own, as well as their own imaginations, and when we finally put two and two together, we see we don't have a thing in common other than good sex. Whatever the reason, the relationship that was based solely on vain imagination goes south, and even if we don't care that much for the other party, we are still attached, and the break hurts. Depending on the level of attachment is what level of pain that will be experienced. Then we develop defense mechanisms, so we won't get hurt like that again. Right or wrong, the first response to anything that causes any sort of pain is to be mindful of doing it again. When something hurts, we don't want to repeat that. Yet we do, time and time again.

If we never learn better, then we can't expect to do and eventually be better. We will repeat the same behavior over and over until we have new information to work with. God, as the good father he is, wants us to be happy, whole, and well equipped to deal with life however it's presented to us. God is the remedy to everything that may have hurt us. We've become great actors and have learned how to fake our way through life, slowly becoming something other than ourselves. Yet the further we slip away from our true selves, the deeper we sink into more damage and pain. We rinse and repeat through life causing so much unneeded pain and hurt on all involved. When we allow God to be our God, he accepts us just as we are. God will show us what a quality relationship, in any aspect, is all about. God loves us, and the first and foremost relationship he wants to help us understand is the relationship with ourselves. The better we understand ourselves and why we do what we do, the better we can become at being us, and the cycle of hurt and being hurt can be resolved.

The more we live this life, and the more experiences we have, the more we develop into who we are. We've had relationships in which we give everything we have. We've had relationships in which we take and take. We've had relationships in which we've been the cause of the hurt and damage, and we've had relationships in which we received the hurt and damage. Every relationship is unique to itself. The only constant in any relationship is the fact that two things that once were separate are now joining together as one. I used to think all women are the same. The more I matured, I noticed it wasn't the women; rather, it was me bringing the same attitude as well as the hurt and pain I've received into something new that had nothing to do with the last. The only thing that was the same about anything was me. I repeated the same behavior that doomed my last relationship, and guess what happened? That one went south too. It wasn't the women that were the same; it was me repeating the same behavior with different women and getting the same result.

How many of us haven't matured into understanding we may be part of the problem? When I was going through my divorce, my ex would always go to get advice from her mom, which is what most women do with someone they trust. The only problem was that her mom was married and divorced five times. I begged my ex to get advice elsewhere. I always got the response, "You just don't like my mom." Not true; I liked my mother-in-law a lot. We went on a lot of family vacations together, and we had some awesome late-night talks. We got along great. But the problem was that my ex was seeking advice from her on a subject her mom had failed at. If your mom has been married and divorced that many times, she may not be very good at being married, and she may not be the best person to ask advice from on that subject. Thankfully, God showed me that I also had some issues I needed to work out before my next romantic relationship. I'm still a work in progress too.

All relationships take work. We've been taught what we know by the experiences we've had. Some are good experiences, and some are not so good. With each relationship, we have to ask ourselves if we have learned anything. Are we still immature and jumping from one romance to another, all the while bringing the same dysfunction as if it were luggage? Are we scared to start any new relationships, especially a romantic one, because we just couldn't take another broken heart, especially if that's the only experience we've had with relationships? Or are we digging in our heels and working through whatever situation arises together with our significant other, because relationships are hard and we're both willing to put in the work? Whatever our individual situation may be, there's a relationship being offered by our Creator that fits one and all, no matter what level of maturity we're on.

I remember a preacher saying once that if we can't get along down here, then we're going to hate heaven. There seems to be a lot of truth to that, seeing how hard of a time we have at sustaining relationships here and now. Our Creator is constantly trying to get us to agree to a relationship with him so he can teach us how to have them with others. I believe we are hesitant about having a relationship with God because of the pain and hurt we've experienced from our human relationships. I can't trust what I see and feel, so how on earth could I trust something I can't see or feel? We may go to church and play the part, but do we really have a father-child relationship with our Creator? Only we can answer that question.

We are alive because God allows it. Our Creator created us for the very reason of having a relationship with him. He created us because he chose to. God loves being a father, and he wants nothing more than to be a father to us. Yet with the gift of our free will, we must accept that offer. As we touched on earlier, a relationship is two things becoming one. We must allow that union to occur. Just like in every relationship, there will be times when we disagree. There will be arguments. There will be ups and downs. Yet, through it all, we can rest assured that our God is perfect and whatever he does he does for our benefit. We get our earthly relationships confused with our heavenly Father. We are two imperfect beings trying to reach perfection. God is perfect, trying to raise us up to his level (1 Corinthians 6:14 NIV).

God loves us, and once we realize the power in that statement and put all our trust and faith in it, we will see life for the gift it is. We've developed our ideas of relationships by what we've experienced in the here and now from other broken people just like us. When we accept God as God, and put him in his rightful place (Romans 10: 9-11 NIV). We have started a new and exciting life, alongside the one who created it. When we experience life the way it was meant to be lived, there will be no doubt about the beauty of it. God puts the life in living, and takes all the pressure off being alive. God not only wants to be, but has the power to be our anything and everything if we allow it. Life takes time. Allow God to be your God, and allow him to take you to heights you've never imagined, as you become the best version of yourself.

The foundation of any relationship is trust. Trust takes a lot of time to build and seconds to tear down. When our trust is broken, we close ourselves off so we don't get hurt again. Some of us have given up or built such a strong wall around ourselves that it couldn't possibly be breached, and that's not a healthy way to live. Really, it's not living at all; that's just existing. God wants us to experience life living it, not by just trying to survive. He wants to shower us with love, and all he asks is for our trust so we can build a strong, healthy relationship together. God has promised to take care of everything pertaining to us, and he will prove it time and time again (Philippians 4:19 NIV), if we stay focused on the main focus, which is God.

"Whoever believes in him shall not perish but have eternal life" (John 3:16 NIV). I used to think, That's it? That's all I must do is believe? Well, I'm good then. Of course, I realize now that believing in something is a process. Belief is a machine that has a lot of gears to make it work. Trust, faith, and confidence are just a few of those. If one part gets damaged, it affects the whole mechanism. If I believe in something, first I have to accept the fact it exists, then have confidence it is what it is, then have faith in what I'm confident exists, and finally trust that all the information is true and accurate, which in turn forms my belief.

All the moving parts work in unison to form a whole. In our individual lives in experiencing what we've learned about relationships, all we've discovered so far is that they're hard to maintain and can cause a lot of pain if not managed correctly, so we develop all sorts of schemes to get what we want out of relationships, then getting out before we get hurt and damaged. God wants to teach us what a real relationship is, so we can in turn use the proper tools when creating our own relationships. No schemes and tricks, just a quality relationship with our Creator as he teaches us the truth. Like our belief machine, the main functioning part is trust. With us being so damaged and hurt, it takes a lot for us to offer our trust to a Creator whom we've never seen or met, but we believe he exists and have put faith and confidence in him, so the next and most important step is trust.

Back to my dogs. The training is easy, because they get used to their routines. All I do is the same thing around the same time every day, and they follow it. They don't question if it's going to happen; they've gotten to the point where they expect it to happen, because I've shown them day in and day out how I do things, and how they can expect them to be done. We need to get to that same level of understanding with our Creator. The more time we spend with him, the more we will see we can trust him as we see how he operates. Truth be told, only God knows what God is going to do next. God is so creative, and he will make things happen that will blow our minds. We get hung up on trusting the process when we should be trusting God. We can trust that God is who he says he is and that he will do what he says he will. Like me training my dogs, the more we experience God, the more we see we can trust him. Our "I believe" will be turned into "I know." I know I can trust God, because he's come through with what he's said he will do.

Now, not only do I believe, but I also know what I believe in is fact. Just like my dogs knowing what time they get fed, the more we give to God, the more he can show us the truth. It's truly all about a relationship. Do we trust God when he says not to worry about anything we need? Do we trust God when he says he's God? Do we trust God when he says he loves us? Ask yourself those questions, and truthfully answer yourself what you believe. Only you can determine how much of a relationship you have with our Creator. It all stems from how much trust we are willing to invest in God. Some of us have made it our whole life, some of us are learning to, and some of us don't seem to care either way. The level of belief and quality of relationship we have with our Creator is solely up to each one of us individually. The choice is ours to make, and I pray we choose wisely.

May God bless you and yours.

Chapter 4
LIGHT SWITCH

I've lived at my present house for some time now, and I would like to think I know it well. When I first moved in, I had no clue what switch did what. As I was learning which switch operated what, I updated many switches to newer versions. I didn't bother with changing around which switch did what, but I knew what they did even if there wasn't much logic involved, so don't fix what isn't broken, right? I remember when I first moved in and didn't have a good understanding of the layout, much less which switch did what, that it made roaming around in the dark interesting. Before I knew which switch controlled which light, I couldn't walk straight to the switch I knew to turn on the light I wanted. Now, after years of living here, I can navigate fairly well, even with a blindfold on.

I was having dinner with a friend of mine at his house the other day, and we stayed a little later than we normally do. I've been over to his house quite a few times, but always in the daylight, and because he lives a little further away and more in the country, and traffic can be quite bad at certain times, we plan our times to visit around the traffic. We normally leave either before or after the times the turnpike is jammed. This one evening, we stayed late to avoid the traffic, and it turned pretty dark by the time we left. I'd never been there when it was that dark before, and let me tell you, when it's dark outside in the country, it's pitch-black. There's no reference of light, no lamps, no nothing. Maybe the moon was hiding that particular night, but I remember I couldn't see anything, and what I thought I knew about the walk back to my car was completely off. I was bumping around into trash cans and recycling cans. I almost twisted my ankle off tripping on a garden hose. I think I stepped in every hole in his yard, and when I finally made it to my car, I couldn't have been more elated. Thank goodness.

I've been in some form of construction most of my life, and recently I've found that working maintenance in buildings is much better than being outside in the blazing sun. The last job I had working maintenance was at a pretty big facility with a lot of nooks and crannies, and there was a huge maze of tunnels and mechanical rooms that one could get lost in pretty easily, which I did a few times when I first started. I remember that once, one of my co-workers and I were way down in the belly of the building fixing some lights, and he had to go back up and get some parts we needed. After he left, I was fooling with one of the lights and accidentally touched some wires together and blew the breaker, and just like that I was in complete darkness. I tried to be patient and wait for my co-worker to come back, but I started to hear all kinds of scurrying sounds around me, and I thought, "Screw this, I'm out!" I started to walk toward what I thought was the exit, but it turned out I was wrong, and I was only going deeper into the pitch-black building. After bumping my head on numerous pipes and bouncing off of randomly stored boxes, I thought I would just go back the way I came. The only problem was that I couldn't tell where I came from. I was lost. Isn't this great? I'm lost in a building in pitch-black darkness with no clue where I am, not to mention all kinds of critters scurrying around. If I'd had my phone, I could have tried to call someone, or at least I could have had some light. Finally, after what seemed forever, my co-worker came back, and I could hear him calling out. Wow. I had really veered off course. I called back out to him and told him to keep talking so I could follow his voice back. He turned on a lamp he had, and then I could see how far I had wandered and how to get back there. What on earth was I thinking? I was nowhere near where I had been or needed to be. I made my way back, and every time I had to venture back down to those tunnels, I went a little more prepared.

Darkness is just the absence of light. With no light or light source, we can expect to be in the dark. How well we function in the dark depends on what we've learned in the light. I can roam around my house perfectly fine in the dark, because I've gotten so accustomed to my layout. My memory is still somewhat good enough to remember what's where, and as long as my son doesn't leave his shoes in the middle of the floor, I have a good understanding about how to maneuver through my house. At my friend's house in the country, I haven't been there enough and explored that environment enough to have a good working knowledge of his layout. Sure, I've been there a couple times, but I haven't paid enough attention to know exactly what's where. Deep in the tunnels of the building I used to work at, I had only been in them a couple times and always with someone else, so it was easy to follow them. Eventually I would have learned more about the layout and would have been able to navigate by myself, but that would have taken time and experience, and I wasn't there long enough to learn that much.

We just had a hurricane come through where I live, and even though it was labeled a hurricane, and met the criteria that we use to label it a hurricane, it wasn't actually that bad. I've been through quite a few hurricanes, and when I hear the word *hurricane*, I think back to some of the more severe storms that really shook my house. This one was just a little wind and rain. By the time it got to us, it had probably lost its hurricane strength, and it was more like a heavy rain cloud with some wind gusts.

Sometimes our life feels the same way. I often listen to various preachers and sermons on YouTube. I've gotten so used to hearing the stereotypical phrases and words that they've gotten stale and repetitive. They've lost their punch. One of the most overused church phrases I hear is when someone is "in a storm." Yes, there are certain times in our lives when we go through things that are way out of our control. However, if you think about it, everything is out of our control; all we do is make our choices on how we deal with things. But sometimes in life we go through times when no matter what we try to decide or choose, nothing goes according to our plans, and it feels as though we are spinning out of control. That would certainly qualify as being in a storm. Yet we often use the phrase "in a storm" for when something doesn't go according to our plans or life goes a little sideways.

The longer we're alive, the more we see how things can go wrong from time to time. Stuff just happens sometimes, and it's not because of a satanic attack. There's no violent storm approaching. The choices we've made in life sometimes just don't work. Our cars break down, our laptops break down, our stuff just breaks down from time to time. It's just stuff; there's no life-giving value to any of it. Let's start calling it what it is. My stuff broke because it's made cheaply in some foreign country. We get so used to hearing the same phrases over and over, so we categorize everything into one convenient term. I've had a few bad days, so I must be in a storm of life. I made a few bad choices, and they have finally grown from sowing to reaping, so I must be in a storm. My kids are acting up, so I must be in a storm. I could go on.

If I don't have the right information on something, then I can't make an informed decision on how I need to deal with it. Storms are a real thing and affect us all, yet when we continuously label everything a storm, it loses its value. Sometimes what we label storms aren't storms at all, and when we call it a storm, we devalue what it is. We miss the point of why we're going through these things because we file it as a storm of life, instead of finding the true meaning of why we're experiencing what we're experiencing, all we do is try to survive until the storm passes.

God uses scenarios of all sorts to teach us and mature us into adults. The only way we learn is through experience. God is our good father, and he is constantly teaching us. He is constantly loving us and constantly trying to get the truth to us. This requires a lot of patience on God's part, because we rarely see what's what. We have to be taught and retaught the same lesson, because we just don't get it.

The more time we spend with God, the more we see how he operates, and we can see his agenda in trying to raise his children. Sometimes God shakes us up in our lives, but that's just to get our attention. He's not trying to make us hunker down and hope for the best; he wants to grab our attention and make us attentive to what he is trying to teach us. If we continue to just call it a storm, we won't open our eyes to what's really going on. We lose the value of the lesson he wants to teach us, because we're not recognizing it for what it is. A storm is something we have no control over; a lesson is something designed to help us grow and mature as we learn something we didn't know before, and it makes us a better person. A storm just batters us till it's over, with no value whatsoever. Sometimes they seem the same on the surface, but how we react to them is different.

I can cruise around my house in the dark or in the light because I've spent enough time in it to know exactly what's what and where everything is. I fumbled around in the dark at my friend's house because I had only been there a few times, and not in the dark. I got lost in the building I worked at, because I had never been down there in the basement by myself, and it was pitch-black. It's easy to discount lessons for what they are and just file things away, but in the end, we're missing the point. Learning lessons from God feels like walking around in the dark. How do I know God will provide for me if I never need anything? How do I know God is a healer and will heal me if need be if I'm never sick? How do I know God is God if I never realize my need for a God? There are some lessons that are quite easy and that we pass with ease because we've been there and done that, and we know exactly what to expect. Some lessons will be a little harder; we sort of know what to expect, but there's some information coming at us we need to decipher to complete the test. Some lessons will be absolutely frightening. We haven't ever experienced anything like this before, and we have no clue how it's going to end up; all we can do is rely on God that he is God and that he won't let us down.

Even as I write this, I find myself in God's school. I'm not in a storm; I'm not being cursed by the devil. There's nothing odd about what I'm going through, other than I've never been through it before. I've spent enough time with God to realize what this is. The Bible tells us, after you've done everything to stand, stand (Ephesians 6:13). I truly get that right now. I am at my wits' end. I know exactly what God has asked me to and what not to do; it's doing it that's the hard part. I've done all right in most of it, but I've dropped the ball in some as well. Isn't that what a test is all about? Lessons are designed to strengthen what needs strengthening and reinforce what we say we know. Today I was so stressed because I'm on the very edge of total disaster. I have my idea of what needs to be done, but it goes against what God has told me to do. I was on the verge of giving up and going back to what I know. Just like when we're fumbling around in the dark, our first inclination is to go back the way we came. We know where we've come from, and we know what to expect. There is a certain amount of comfort in that, but it doesn't help in strengthening anything. God wants us to mature and evolve. If we continue to do the same thing over and over, there's no growth whatsoever. Sure, we're comfortable and content, but we stay on the same level forever, neither increasing or decreasing, just existing.

We are constantly growing and evolving into something all the days of our lives. At times our lives are like our environment, in which we are comfortable and content. Other times are like being at a friend's house and being only sort of familiar with our surroundings. Lastly, at other times, we are in utter darkness and have no clue where we are or how to find our way. We may be on any one of these levels, but the common denominator in all of these levels is that God is always there. God is always willing and ready to teach us, and knowing that God is God and that he is faithful and true has to be the most important lesson any of us could hope to learn.

We learn through experience, and once we experience something, it becomes fact in our mindset. God is trying to get us from "Maybe I believe," to "I know and believe that God is God." How does he do that? Through teaching and testing, just like we learned when we attended school. Storms come and go, and they certainly tear stuff up in our lives, but when we realize that the proverbial storm is just God shaking up our lives so he can teach us something we need to know, it makes enduring the lessons so much easier. Then we realize there's purpose behind what we're going through. I don't just put up hurricane shutters and wait for the storm to pass; I try to be attentive to what I'm being taught and learn the lessons that make me a more mature person. So, let's start calling it what it is. We miss so much beneficial information if we just label our trials a storm and only wait them out, when it's actually God knocking on our hearts and minds asking us to open up and get ready for a spiritual lesson.

May God bless you and yours.

Chapter 5

CIVILIZED SOCIETY

We truly have a marvelous God whom we can call Father, if we so choose. I hope we have all come to that understanding in our individual lives and are experiencing the blessings that come along with that relationship. Everything that comes from our God is good, holy, and true. That's who God is, not just what he does. God cannot give us something he doesn't have, and there is no evil whatsoever in our Creator. On the other hand, God can give us plenty of what he does have, which is love. How God shows us that love is what we sometimes have a hard time understanding. How could a loving God allow such evil and sin as we see every day in this world? Why do bad things happen to good people? The list goes on, but the question remains the same. How can something so ultimately holy seem to turn a blind eye to this cesspool we call home? How is that even possible? Light always trumps darkness; we can just turn on a light switch and see for ourselves how quickly darkness goes away. So, what's the problem? Why is everything getting worse instead of getting better?

These are solid questions for sure. Solid questions deserve solid answers, and we seem to be fresh out of those. All we do now is look up everything about anything on the internet, without using one atom of our own brains. But if we are truly seeking answers to life's puzzling questions, of which there are many, we'd be wise to start with the source of all creation, our God. And the beauty of it all is that's exactly what God wants. God is a great Father toward his children, and he has all the true information about anything we could ever hope to think about.

Throughout our history, society after society has come up with its own ideals and systems, which they put in place to accommodate their opinions of how they believe life is meant to be lived. Some civilizations set up governments that have total control over their citizens. Some have set up systems that have a king to rule over its people. Some have given the citizens power by having them choose who will rule over them. Some civilizations have set their own religious guidelines, some strict, some lax. The common denominator is that they've set up their government based on whatever they feel works for them. Since all ideals have pros and cons, to say one is better than the other is not very wise. The truth is that there will never be a perfect government until our God comes to reclaim what's his. The reason we can never have a perfect government here on earth is because of us, our sinful selves. We are too easily swayed by our egos, our pride, and our lust for power, and we can never have that nirvana that so many of us yearn for. How nice would it be to be able to smile at someone without them looking at you like you're off your rocker or questioning your motives. I long for the day when I can just be me, happy and content to be alive. But the way things are on this earth, that day isn't coming, right?

Here in the United States, the system we've created is wonderful in theory, but its implementation is less than desirable. We have a great idea of how a civilized society should function, but because of the greed and lust of the powerful few, that idea is just a dream. We can pretend we're fine, but in reality, we're on a leaky boat three-quarters full of water in the middle of the ocean. We have reduced the meaning of life down to working, paying bills, buying things on credit (which will lead to more bills), owning as much useless stuff as we can, saving what little bit of money we can to support us when we can't work anymore, and then peacefully moving from earth to heaven when God calls us home. What an exciting adventure that sounds like.

Recall that phrase, "When God calls us home." Isn't this earth our home? Well, Jesus taught us that we are "not of this world" (John 17:16, paraphrase). No, this earth is not our home; we're just traveling here for a while till we make the move to our mansion in eternity with our Creator. We are subject to whatever our civilized society has instilled as far as government, but it's not who we are. We are children of God and subject to his laws and truth, and that's what we are. We were made by his love, and we separate ourselves from that love when we choose not to live in it. God has been trying to reconnect us to himself ever since, and he offers us his redemption time and time again. God knows what we are and what it takes to bring us back home. The problem is that we think we know, but we don't.

When I think about great civilizations, I think back to the ancient Romans. They left behind some impressive architecture as well as some good ideas on how to run a government. Of course, they did have a rather violent society, and they had a system of slavery installed, so not all their ideas were good. Yet they were the ones who gave us the republic form of democratic government, which has been imitated and implemented by many civilizations since. As civilized as the Romans seemed, they nevertheless thought of anyone who didn't agree with their beliefs as barbarians and less than themselves. When their civilization finally met its end, the world did go into a time we refer to as the Dark Ages, mostly because the most powerful government at that time, good or bad, was no longer around to lead an organized society. So, whether their government was good or bad, they were still the leading society at their time in history, and when they were no longer in power and a source of stability in an unstable environment, its citizens scattered and were left to their own devices.

Juvenal, one of the earlier historians of Roman life, writes in his poem about the declining civilization, "Two things only the people anxiously desire: bread and circuses." The Roman emperors had figured out the key to keeping their citizens content, and that boiled down to keeping them busy and happy. As a result, they gave the poor free bread, and everyone, poor and rich alike, attended the many festivals and games throughout the year. Bread and circuses: feed them and keep them entertained. That all seems well and good, but when the free ride is over and society has to learn how to provide for themselves, if they have always relied on someone or something else to meet their needs, they will not have the know-how to do what they need to do.

Society after society has taken what they've learned from other civilizations and have used what they think is fair and right and tweaked what they think will be more beneficial to their own ideas on how a government should be set up and run. Civilizations have come and gone. Ideas have been implemented, some that worked, and some that got scrapped as better ideas were thought up. Some societies have run their civilization through military force. Some have given its citizens say, and some have given its citizens no say at all. One thing these governments have in common is that they understand that we as humans feel more comfortable when we are being led and guided. I know I do. Life is so much easier when some of the more important choices about life and living are laid out in front of us, and all we must do is choose which direction we want to go. We've made some good choices and some not-so-good choices; we've figured out what works and what doesn't for us, but in the end we all need laws and some form of stability. So, we have chosen people to do that for us, and we call that our government.

When we are born, we have no choice of which government we are born under. Laws are already in place, the government has already determined how it rules its people, and here we come. Now, when we get older and are more developed intellectually, we can choose to stay under that governmental authority or look for another. The same goes for us. We were born into sin, and have no say in that. The sin is already here, passed from one generation to the next, traced all the way back to the first humans ever created. The good news is that Jesus broke that cycle, and just as sin entered the world through the first man, forgiveness now comes through Jesus. So now we have another option. Living in the sin we were born into has now become a choice instead of a law. Yes, we are born into sin, but the more developed we become, we have the option to return to a holy God for redemption, or continue in our sin to death.

When we choose to allow God to be our God, we have signed off for him to show us the truth about life and living. Let me begin by saying if we aren't following God, what we are doing is not living and has no life value in it whatsoever. Our worldly system revolves around fending for ourselves and doing whatever needs to be done to provide for ourselves and our family. We work like pack animals, just to work more. We work hard to earn a buck so that we can get what we need. Our system revolves around money, and without it there is no system. We have great ideas, but they mostly revolve around money. Without money there is no power, without power we can't make a good living, and without living there is no life. Right? Our system has its share of good points, but the fuel that feeds it will never be enough to meet its insatiable hunger. The more money we make, the more taxes we pay. The higher wage we earn just raises the prices of the goods we need to survive. It's a system that will eventually fail because of unchecked greed and lust for power.

When we follow God, life with him is different. God comes looking for us, offering us all an invitation to follow him, but it's our choice if we do or don't. For those of us who choose to follow him, God is trying to teach us the one true system and one true government. Yet some of us find it so difficult to trust and believe in God. First off, God is a spirit, and he relates to us through our spirits. We need to learn how to recognize when God is talking to us. The more we practice listening for his voice, the more we learn how to hear him. God is our Father, and he wants to teach his children the truth about life and living. The more we grow from spiritual babies into what we are now, the more we learn about his spiritual system. Without God teaching us, the best we can hope for in learning spiritual matters is an educated guess, unless we are taught and shown the truth.

This is exactly what God is trying to accomplish in all of us. He wants to raise children from babies to grown adults. God is teaching us what we don't know, and just like here on earth, we need to learn from experience and be educated by someone who knows what we're trying to learn. In the physical world, we know what we can see and feel as fact. What we don't know is spiritual truths. We cannot see or feel a spirit, so we need someone who understands the spiritual world to teach us what we need to know. This teacher is Jesus Christ. What did he teach? Read the Bible, and you'll learn. The New Testament is primarily the written accounts of his life and teachings.

The Bible is God's written Word, but it doesn't become real to us until we experience it. We need to see and feel it in our everyday lives. Once we've felt it and seen it, then we can't deny its existence, and if we choose to, then we are liars, and the truth is not in us (see 1 John 2:4). This is what God is trying to teach us. He has given us his Word in the Bible, and he gives us its meaning when he brings us through life experiences that we can see and feel. Therefore, the truth is now in us whether we accept it or not. After all, what better teacher could we have than the one who literally wrote the book?

God is trying to teach us the meaning of life and living. The system we have set up for ourselves here on earth is not even close to the one true system that we will all eventually come under when we move from this life to eternity. Here in this existence, we are under the law of time. We have a certain amount of time available to us to live as we please. Eternity, where God lives, is a timeless existence, not restrained to limits as we are now. God is a just God and has given us covenant after covenant, basically meaning he made deals with us. If you do this. I'll do this type thing. God has offered us all forgiveness, and the option of becoming reborn, and in doing so, we will live in eternity with God, as him as our God and us as his people. This is the current covenant available to anyone who accepts it. The system we live under now, is God cleansing us of sin. The system to come will be us worshiping the one true God in his paradise forever and ever. Do not fall into the thinking of this is all there is. Friends, this is only the beginning.

God is trying to prepare us for eternity and his system, but we cannot learn if we refuse to be taught. When God comes knocking with his life lessons in hand, we fail to recognize them for what they are. Why? Because his lessons and his truth go totally against our system and our idea of how life is supposed to be lived, and we don't humble ourselves enough to be taught the truth. Some of us have constructed very comfortable lives for ourselves. We've worked hard and gathered up more than enough money. We've built huge homes. We've bought the finest things for ourselves. We've worked this earthly system to a tee and provided very well for ourselves. The problem? There is not a single drop of life in anything we've worked so hard to attain;

At the end of the day, it's all wasted time spent on worthless items. True life comes from God and God alone. God is trying to teach us the truth, but if we're too comfortable living out a brief existence in our comfortable lie, then we have quite the problem.

Our worldly system has been developed as an exact opposite of the true system. God doesn't expect us to know what the true system is, but does expect us to be willing to be taught. Without faith, it's impossible to please God (Hebrews 11:6), because if we lack faith, we are telling God we don't trust him. You have to start somewhere, and it's not too late to start our journey with God as our leader, provider, and Father. God will teach us the truth, if we only allow it. It's hard, very hard—in fact, it will be the hardest thing we've ever done—but in the end, it will be worth it, and what's more, we will get better at it.

The truth is not in this world. We can never learn the truth by ourselves; we can only learn it from God. God is trying to teach us the truth and to have us experience more and more of it. As long as we allow God to work in our lives, the more truth he can show us. But again, it's very difficult to do something that totally contradicts the system we have known since birth, and it will shake us to our very core. Nevertheless, in order to make something new, the old must be replaced, right? Faith is the key. Trust that God is God and will not allow us to fail as long we listen and do what he says.

I am living proof that God is God and that he will do what he says he will, which is be whatever we need whenever we need it. I can attest to the fact that life is more than working just so we can survive. My prayer for anyone who reads this is to give God a try. We wouldn't be alive without him, so if we have breath in our lungs, let's look for him as hard and as long as he looked for us. Only then will we know and experience the truth about life and living. It will be by far the toughest, hardest thing you've ever experienced, but when the lesson is over, you will be so glad you learned it. There is so much we need to learn; I pray we stay humble and faithful to our Creator as he brings us into his life-giving knowledge.

    May God richly bless you and yours.

Chapter 6
ISOLATION

In all of the true believers' lives, there will come a time when we are kept apart, hidden, or isolated. This will be a time of communion between ourselves and God, and nothing else. This is meant to enforce our beliefs as we spend time together with our Creator, as well as prepare us for what purpose God has for us to accomplish. When we first enter this phase of our existence, we far too often miss the beauty of it. We feel as though God is punishing us for a hidden sin we didn't repent for, or God has forgotten or abandoned us. We feel as if something is wrong, other than we are exactly where we're supposed to be doing what we're supposed to be doing.

God creates methodically, and nothing is random or out of order. In these times of isolation, there is a greater cause than what we know at that time. "At that time Jesus was led by the Spirit into the desert to be tempted by the devil. He fasted for forty days and forty nights and afterwards was hungry" (Matthew 4:1 KJV). Jesus was being brought to the territory of the enemy and was about to undertake the first of many spiritual fights against Satan. How did he prepare himself? He was brought to a place where it was just him and our God. Jesus denied his body anything and fed his spirit by being alone with God, in essence taking the power away from the body, while raising up his spirit. The devil came to him and tempted him with physical power, but Jesus, being strong in the spirit, denied the devil and his temptation by staying true to the spirit, which was made strong by his fasting. Jesus took the time he was isolated and used it to strengthen what needs strengthening for the fight that was coming.

There are many synonyms for the word isolation, and there are many reasons why God has set us apart when he does. Moses had quite a start to his life (Exodus 2 NIV). The story in a nutshell: the Egyptians had feared the Israelites because of their numbers, so they enslaved them and to slow them down from multiplying, the pharaoh had ordered that every male Hebrew child born should be killed. When Moses was born, his mother hid him until she couldn't hide him anymore, so she put him in a basket into the river where she knew the pharaoh's daughter would come to bathe. The daughter found him and had mercy on him and raised him as her own. God knew the plans he had for Moses, and hid him until he was prepared for the task that God had appointed for him to do.

In story after story, there are many accounts of people who have been isolated and kept apart, yet that's not the point. Finish their stories and we can see the why behind it. God has his reasons why he isolates and keeps us separate, and he has his reasons why he doesn't fill us in at that time. When we find ourselves in times of isolation, know there is a greater purpose as to why. We are getting ready to embark on something we don't have a reference for, and do things we probably don't know how to do. It's step by step with God, and that's done intentionally. One, so it doesn't overwhelm us, and two, we become stronger after each step. Look at the story of the prodigal son (Luke 15:11-32 KJV). One of the main focuses of that story is if you get too much too soon, before we are responsible enough to be responsible with it, it very well could destroy us. God wants to bless all of us with blessings we can't imagine, but he also wants our character to be solid enough for us to handle it.

God wants us all to be healthy, wealthy and wise, but that takes effort. God doesn't want his children uninformed, destitute, and sick, yet that's where a lot of us find ourselves because we refuse to do it the way God would teach us to. We've all fallen into the category of the prodigal son. We've gotten too much too soon, and eventually it's all lost because we only have the knowledge and strength to get it, and no understanding of what it takes to keep it. Jesus was led by the spirit to be tempted by the devil. Did Jesus know this? Jesus for sure knows how to listen and follow his Father's voice, but did he know what was going to happen when he got there? He was led by the spirit into the desert is all the information we get. Jesus fasted for forty days and forty nights. Was this by necessity, only for the fact that there's no food in the desert, and Jesus was following the commands of his father, and if he leads to where there's no food, then so be it. The Bible doesn't clarify why Jesus fasted; it just says he did. If Jesus knew what he was getting ready to face or if he didn't, he still followed God's leading and endured his time of isolation until the purpose was made clear. The spirit brought him to the desert, and prepared him for what was coming, just like he does us if we stay the course and don't abandon the process.

God is leading us, if we allow, and God knows the beginning and ending. There is a reason behind times of isolation, and it could very well be as simple as just God allowing us to catch our proverbial breath and take a break from the fast-paced world we live in. Just as there are so many synonyms for isolation, there are a multitude of reasons why, and only God knows why. It's our duty, just like our lord Jesus, to follow our God's direction one step at a time.

Our own intellect hurts us more than it helps in times of isolation. Feelings of uselessness may set in because our only option is to learn patience as we wait on God. We have good intentions to further the kingdom of our God, but we fail to recognize the importance of what's being built in us, as God has us in a holding pattern. Patience. This one trait is the cornerstone and building block for any and all of the qualities of love. Patience brings another level of understanding to any situation we may face. So many issues could be solved if we took our time to judge the circumstances we find ourselves in instead of rushing to an uninformed conclusion.

God lives in eternity and is not confined to time as we are. We would be wise to realize that God is not only teaching us how to thrive in this existence, he is teaching us his traits and qualities so we know what to expect in the next level of our existence. We have a hard time with learning patience because we know our time is limited, and we understand the need for learning how to be responsible for something, it's just our idea of responsible and God's idea of responsible are usually two different things. This is what God is trying to teach us, his level of thinking and modes of operation. God is raising us up to his level, not sinking down to ours.

We are never more like our God than when we are patiently waiting. God is teaching us the single most important lesson of all when he's teaching us patience, while he has us waiting for what he has us waiting for. It seems like what we're being patient for is never going to happen, and our first thought is to "help" God along in making it happen. We start to slowly drift from having faith in our Maker, to "I'll go ahead and make this happen the way I think it should." When we do this, and some of us have far too often taken things into our own hands. We devalue the whole purpose of the lesson and we will have to retake the test over and over, until we catch on. The sole purpose of God teaching us patience, and stretching us so thin in our waiting is to teach us the valuable lesson of being responsible with power.

When we are choosing to have faith in our God, we are in essence saying, "I am choosing to not use my power to override God's power," and in turn giving him the respect he deserves as the ultimate power he is. True wisdom comes from having the power over something but choosing not to use it. That is God to a tee. He respects the gift he gave us, when he gave us free will, by not making us choose anything. This is the purpose of the waiting season we all go through when we follow God. He is teaching how to be responsible with the power he has given us. We are never more powerful than having the power over something and choosing not to use it.

Just the other day, I was going about my daily business, and thoughts of me just being lazy, and I'm not doing what God has told me to do, or anything for that matter came up. So, I did what I always do when those thoughts come up. I prayed and asked God if that were true. Am I doing enough God? Am I in your will, am I doing what I'm supposed to be doing? The thoughts of uselessness set in. depression was coming on, and I just felt worthless. Then I realized that I'm not using the tools I have been taught to use. I can't stop the temptations and worthless thoughts from coming, but I can control how I process and/or accept them. I fought back like Jesus did, with the word of God. I said to myself, God did bring me here. God has given me the work that I am doing, which is currently waiting on him for step two. And God is leading and I am following (Proverbs 16:9 KJV). And God clarified it when I asked him.

"Am I doing what I'm supposed to be doing?" I asked.

"What are you doing?" God replied.

"Patiently waiting on you for the next step," I said.

And at that very moment a feeling of peace and tranquility literally washed over me, so without God saying a word, I take that as yes, I'm doing exactly what I'm supposed to be doing. Step two is coming, and I'll be prepared and ready for it when it gets here.

"I will sprinkle clean water on you, and you will be clean; I will cleanse you from all your impurities and from all your idols. I will give you a new heart and put a new spirit in you; I will remove from you your heart of stone and give you a heart of flesh" (Ezekiel 36:25-26 NIV). This is God's goal for all of us. How he goes about it is individually tailored to our unique selves. Your experiences will be your experiences and mine will be mine, but the process will be the same. There will be times of brokenness, times of overflowing joy, and times of isolation where it's just you and God. When we read about Jesus' experience in the desert, we can read why he needed to be strengthened. When we read about Moses' story, we can see how God hid him in the very household that wanted him dead, then prepared him in his own isolation to do the awesome work that God had for him to do. There will be times of isolation, and it will feel as though God has forgotten us, but I assure you he hasn't forgotten. He is only preparing us for what's to come. Your story is not over. In fact, it's just the beginning. When isolated, we are being taught patience, endurance, how to use what tools God has already given us. There's multiple reasons God has us isolated when he does, it's our duty to stay faithful in the dark as we do in the light. A new you is being created, and we can thank God he doesn't rush as we like to do. God is creating a clean, washed in the blood perfect version of you that is fit for heaven and the kingdom of God, and it takes the amount of time it takes. Again, we are being prepped for heaven and eternity so what time we invested in the here and now will not be wasted. It may feel as though we're wasting our time, and nothing is being accomplished, but God is God and knows what he's trying to accomplish, it's our only job to agree with him that he knows what he's doing and humble ourselves to the process.

May God richly bless you and yours.

Chapter 7

ABSOLUTELY

As long as there are lawyers in this world, there can never really be concrete law. Our society has set up laws in an attempt to keep order. Laws are just sets of rules that are put in place to keep our society in a functioning order. Without order, everyone would do whatever they felt whenever they felt it. As chaotic as our world already seems to be, could you imagine the kind of chaos that would create? Without laws, there would be no order, and without order, there would be anarchy and constant chaos. Who wants to live like that? Is that even living?

We all live by rules and laws. Parents run their household by whatever moral standards they see fit. Rules and laws are something we constantly contend with, whether it's a moral standard or an actual law that would get the police called on us. What's more, our rules and laws as humans, especially in the United States, are constantly changing and adapting to popular opinion. Think back to prohibition in the early twentieth century. Our society at the time thought it would be wise to ban alcohol, but after years of civil uproar about it, the law was eventually changed to allow what once was banned. The same is happening today. Marijuana has been illegal as long as I can remember, and yet now, with public opinion behind it, and with our scientists and medical professionals learning more information about it, it seems as though it will eventually become legal. What once was considered a crime will soon be accepted in our society.

With our ever-changing opinions and ideals, it really makes it hard to set and enforce any law. Of course, we know what the more severe laws are, like murder for instance, but even then, any decent lawyer can argue the facts and make it hard to prove that the law was broken. So, as long as there are lawyers, no law can be written as concrete fact, at least not in the system of government we've set up for ourselves. We have the laws in place, but enforcing them and proving a person's guilt seems to be the issue. We write law after law after law. We've created so many laws to enforce the laws that were already in place, who could possibly keep up? It's a valiant effort by our society to keep order, but in the end, there's too many rules, and one couldn't possibly keep them all.

Think back to the account of Jesus's life in the Bible. Jesus was up against a system that was so worried about breaking God's laws, a person could hardly breathe without running the risk of breaking one of the many laws they had instituted. They had God's laws, given in the Old Testament, and they continued to pile on human rules in order to keep themselves in what they perceived as God's true law. Only problem? It was unsustainable. Back then, they interpreted remembering the Sabbath and keeping it holy as meaning they shouldn't work. Well, what constitutes work? To them, everything. They had rule upon rule set up so they wouldn't break the first rule. Yet if even one rule was broken, that person would be considered unholy and an outlaw, because they didn't keep the whole law.

I've had animals most of my life: mainly dogs, with a few cats thrown in; I've even been around some farm animals, such as cows, horses, and chickens. Currently, I have two dogs, and for the most part they're great. Just like every animal, every now and again they do what they do and don't care what anyone says, but for the most part, they've learned my way of doing things, and they keep to the program. The two I have now are good enough to let outside without a leash. They listen and obey commands, such as "Come here," and "Sit," so I don't have to worry about them running off and never coming back, or worse, biting someone. They may bark to no end, but neither one of them would hurt anyone.

The dog we had before these two was great except for one thing. We could not for the life of us keep him in our yard. I have a fence that spans the whole backyard, and for where I live, my yard is considered sizable. I walked the entire span time after time, and I could not find any gaps or holes that he could escape from, yet every single time I let him in the yard, he found his way out. He would run the neighborhood, barking at everything and everyone. Not only was it hard to keep him in the yard, getting him to come back inside was quite a chore as well. I tried everything, and my neighbors even pitched in, but nothing we did would ever coax him back in the yard. He came to the front door when he was good and ready, and then eventually he would come inside. It finally got to the point where we could only let him outside on a run with a leash we had set up, but then he just barked and barked like a spoiled child wanting his way, so we eventually gave up on that idea too. We honestly tried everything we could possibly do, but eventually we lost the battle, and we gave him to our neighbors who gave him to someone else. He was a great dog; he just refused to conform to our rules we had set in place. We tried to adapt to him, but we just couldn't, so we had to part company.

Every now and again, when I let my dogs out at night, they have a run-in with raccoons or possums. The older dog has no fear and will run straight at it—at least until she comes whimpering back because the raccoon has bitten or scratched her. One night we even had a huge turtle dig under our fence and make its way toward our house. Both dogs went to inspect, and both came whimpering back. The younger dog had taken quite a bite and was bleeding pretty badly from his paw. We patched him up and had him back on his feet in a few days. I once again walked the fence, and I eventually dug out a trench that ran the length of the fence, and then I filled with concrete the whole run that spans along our canal. I thought it best to do that because I've seen worse than raccoons and turtles show up back there. I'm dealing with cougars and gators, and I don't want anything to hurt my animals.

The main reason I strengthened my fence was not to keep my animals in the yard but to keep predators out. My dogs still have two other spans of fence where they can get out—and trust me, they try. The non-reinforced fence looks like a bombed-out war zone full of craters. They both love to dig, and sometimes I think they dig not because they are trying to escape but because they're bored. Even when someone leaves one of the gates open and the dogs do manage to get out, once I notice and call for them, they come shooting right back. We have a good relationship. They've learned what they can and can't get away with, and for the most part, they keep in line with our rules.

The more we get to know our Creator, the more we can see he's all about order. Nothing that happens can happen out of the order in the way he designed it to work. The very first time we get introduced to our God in Genesis, he's in the process of taking chaos and placing it in order into a functioning system. Everything that was created has a design and function, and it will only function in the order it was meant to. This includes even us, as God's prized creation. We have an order we must follow in order to function. If we don't take in air, we can't follow the first step in making our being work. If we don't make that first step, then the following steps can't function, and the cycle will be incomplete and broken. Order is the key. Every step is working in harmony with the next and last. Where there is order there is functionality; where there is no order there is non-function. When we became separated from our God, we allowed something to disrupt our order that was never meant to be there. We fell out of order and out of sync with our God. Because of sin, God had to rework his order and provide for us a way to stay in order, and that came in the form of laws: the Ten Commandments.

The Ten Commandments are ten basic laws that our God has given us. They are laws not meant to punish but to protect and correct. Just like my concreted fence, the laws that God had given us are for our protection, not confinement. They are designed to help us get back in order and keep us functioning as we grow into a mature, orderly being. When we stay inside the boundaries of the laws, we can find order and harmony. If we choose to live outside the laws, we can only find chaos and anarchy. The Ten Commandments are God's perfect law, and they cover every issue we encounter as human beings. They become imperfect when we put our spin on them. Like the generation of Jesus' time, who made up rule upon rule in order to not break the first rule, when we reinterpret God's commandments, we lose the meaning of the laws in the first place. We cannot live a perfect life; however, we can live an honest life as we try to stay within the law set before us. The more we try to stay within the boundaries, the more we will see why they're there in the first place. God's laws are meant to protect, not condemn and convict.

All of God's Ten Commandments are God's way of telling us to be wary of a given situation. Remember when mom told you not to touch the hot stove, and yet we touched it and found out it's hot and it hurt? The same thing is going on with the Ten Commandments. If we want to live out of balance and out of order, then we may as well live as we see fit. But if we want to live in relative peace and harmony, we need to stay inside the boundaries laid out in the Ten Commandments. Listen to God when he says the proverbial stove is hot, and don't touch it.

Ever since the first two humans fell out of order and harmony, God has been trying to restore balance and order to the chaos we've created. His laws are only a fence meant to protect us from the evils that come from engaging in the behavior that are laid out in his commandments. The choice is ours on how we decide we want to experience this life. If we choose to live outside the boundaries, we have chosen to be our own god, living in the world we've created for ourselves. If we've chosen God and his order, then we will be mindful of his laws. We will most certainly fail time after time, but we're staying mindful and trying not to repeat the same behavior that caused us to fail in the first place. We are on a lifelong journey of maturity and growth. Growth comes from maturing, and maturing comes from growth. Notice the cycle? Work with God as he gets us back in sync and takes us from lawless to the functioning orderly being he created in the first place.

May God richly bless you and yours.

Chapter 8

ONE, THEN TWO, THEN THREE

Whenever we're being taught something, either in a school setting or through life experience, there's a sequence of events that takes place to get us to the point at which we understand what we're being taught. When we learned how to count, we were taught the sequence of numbers that make up our system of mathematics. When we learned the alphabet, we were taught the sequence of letters and their placement in the order of the alphabet. When we learned how to spell, we were taught which letters are used and in what order they are placed to form the words of our language. Whatever we're being taught, there is an order to the way we must be shown for it to make sense.

Even in our physical bodies, there's a sequence of events that take place as we progress from one level to the next. When we were babies, we rolled around, then we progressed to crawling, then to walking, and eventually to running and jumping and everything in between. There's an order that takes place. When we've mastered one level, we progress to the next. It's called maturing and growth. Even the most accomplished person in the world started out knowing nothing about anything until they went through lessons and gained knowledge and understanding through growth and maturing.

Construction is the name of my game. I have been in some form of construction my whole life, from building, facility work, to anything and everything pertaining to building and engineering. I would like to think of myself as above average in the construction field. I've "been there, done that" on quite a range of projects, and while I definitely don't know it all, I've nevertheless got a good grasp on quite a bit. I could fake it till I make it no matter what job I've had. I gained all this from years of trial and error, years of learning different views and processes, years of working with many different people with many different skills.

I remember when I first started, I had no clue about anything. I was just the yard monkey and gofer. It was a needed job, but not a very desirable one. To move from being the trash boy, I needed to learn another skill so I could pass that job on to the next new hire, which I did very quickly. I learned skill after skill. I eventually started my own company, which led to a whole new set of skills I had to learn. I went in thinking I knew everything there is to know about owning my own company. I know how to do what I'm trying to sell to others; it's just as simple as selling the work, doing the work, and getting paid, right? Well, not so much. As headstrong as I was, I had the shock of my young life. There is so much more to running a company than what I thought I knew. Sure, I knew how to do the work in a professional manner and to do it right. What I didn't know was the white-collar aspect of having a business. What I thought I knew was a far cry from the reality of my situation. It took time, effort, and a lot of money to learn how to effectively run a business.

I managed my business for years, going through challenge after challenge, employee after employee, situation after situation. I learned as I went. The more experience I gained, the more effective I became at owning and operating my company. We managed pretty well, but near the end, we became stagnant. We weren't growing, but we weren't dying either. We just seemed to be stuck. I didn't realize it at the time, but I get it now. I was content with where we were. I wasn't putting in any effort to expand; I was just happy being at the level we were at. If it's not broke, don't fix it, right? The problem? We had more and more competition around us, and word-of-mouth only takes someone so far. These other companies had money to burn on advertising, and they either processed their own materials or had deals in place to exclusively use a company's product. Either way I cut it, I hadn't put in effort to grow and adapt to the changing atmosphere. I was content being where we were. I was making enough money to keep the doors open and keep our bills paid, but that was about it. There wasn't much to go around for anything other than the necessities. At the beginning we were making money hand over fist, so what was the problem now?

Years after we shuttered our company, I see exactly what the problem was. I was the problem. I liked things the way they were, and I didn't open up my mind to see the writing on the wall. There was enough work to go around for all of us to make a living; the issue was that more companies were realizing the potential of what we were doing, and they changed their business model to do the same work we were doing. There was a feeding frenzy. It was like when a shark tastes blood in the water. At first there were only three or four companies doing our line of work, but that exploded into twenty or more in what felt like just a few months. They advertised, offered products and services we didn't, and they had the weight of established corporations behind them. The more companies that came in to play, the lower the prices dropped, so our profits were cut in half, if not more. Between those issues and the issue of me not paying attention to the rising costs of materials, gas, wage increases, and overall increases in everything, our business eventually failed. There were things I could have done and some things I should have done to keep my business alive, but after years of highs and lows and everything in between, I was just plain tired. I was broke in every aspect of the word. I had zero money, zero energy, zero anything. I was so worn out after spending year after year doing what had to be done to keep the business profitable and healthy, I couldn't stand another minute of doing it. I quit. I closed the business, sold what I could, and gave away the rest. I just wanted to be done with construction.

After bouncing around for a handful of years and taking quite a few menial jobs, I finally found a good one. I was hired at a performing arts center, which paid great and had the best benefits I've ever had. I really enjoyed that job, and I wish I could have kept it, but God had other plans. I recall some of the shows they would put on and what was entailed in making them happen. If I had never worked there, I would never have guessed how much is involved just to put on a two-hour show. In the days leading up to the show, we would go through all the rooms and areas that would be used backstage and make sure everything was functioning and in working order. The act would show up with all their actors and gear, and it took an army of people to get stuff set up according to their needs. Lighting, cameras, props, sets. The whole process from start to finish was quite an impressive coordination of logistical expertise. I watched it happen time and time again, but watching and making it happen are two different things. There is no way I could coordinate all that without formal training. Yet I'm sure that at one point, those who made the magic happen for show after show were in the same spot as I was, before they learned their craft.

In the days leading up to a show, there would be a tornado of people buzzing around, doing everything that needed doing. We just stayed out of the way unless we got a call for something that was broken. If we wanted to see the show, we could usually get free tickets or at least a cheaper-than-advertised price. I was lucky enough to be working during most of the shows so I could watch for free and get paid for it.

I remember for one particular show, they had this one lighting prop that they struggled with all week long to get to work. Even during the show, they didn't know if it would work or not, so they just went ahead and hoped for the best. When it was time during the show to use that particular prop, it went off without a hitch, and truthfully, it was pretty impressive. I see why they paid so much attention to it. It really made the show pop, and I could see how different it would have been if it hadn't been used. When everything is said and done, the work involved was worth the payoff. It wowed the audience and gave the show another level of showmanship.

We're never more like our Creator than when we are creating and moving. There's a certain level of self-satisfaction involved as well. It just feels good. When we make something out of an idea we had, it's a great feeling to see what we envisioned come together. The same is true when we're growing and learning. It's very satisfying to expand our knowledge and learn new and exciting things. The other side of that coin, though, is when we seem to be stuck, going through the same motions, day in and day out. We run the risk of becoming depressed and uninterested. If we're not careful we lose hope, and without hope there is no life.

It's sad to say, but the majority of people in this world seem to be stuck in neutral. They are neither moving forward or backward; they are just staying planted right where they are. God knows this too, and that's why he is constantly trying to help us. Truthfully, most of us don't even recognize God's help when it comes. We may think our world is coming to an end because our status quo gets upended and life gets shaken to its core. I remember a pastor saying that when it's time for baby eagles to get out of the nest and learn to fly, the mama eagle will make the nest so uncomfortable for the eaglet that it will eventually leave the nest and learn what it has to in order to survive. With that same logic, we could say that God does that to us sometimes as well. Like me and my business, my refusal to adapt to the changing world and staying content with what I had, a closed mind lacks perspective. My business is now out of business because I wouldn't allow it to grow.

Everything God does is for our benefit. That includes making us uncomfortable enough until we finally accept a different perspective. It takes a lot to pry open a closed mind, but I guarantee God has the right crowbar. God wants us to be happy and enjoy this gift of life. Anything that becomes stale and stuck will eventually die. Leave a banana on your counter for a week, and you'll see what I mean. What started a bright greenish-yellow will turn into a black mushy mess if it's left alone. God doesn't want any of us to become that banana. God will work with us as much or as little as we want him to.

God will give us opportunities to grow and mature, but his methods are like that mama eagle. We don't recognize it as love; instead, we think it's punishment for some sin we did (or are doing). We're going along with our daily grind, and then kaboom! Life goes sideways. When that happens, the first thing we do is try to make sense of it, and far too often the easiest solution is to blame God and assume we're being punished. This couldn't be further from the truth. When we read the Bible, we can see who took the punishment meant for mankind. Jesus took all our sins and the punishment for them on the cross.

We're not being punished; we're being nudged to get off our lazy butts and start living life again. God didn't create this whole big world and everything in it for us to sit and stagnate in it. If we believe we were created in the image of God, our Creator, then we are at our best when we're creating, learning new things, giving and receiving love, helping our brothers and sisters, and enjoying being alive. We're at our worst when we've become stuck and are neither alive or living, just existing and surviving.

Our lives are a gift to us from the God who created them. Gifts are meant to be enjoyed, not to be hidden and forgotten.

We sometimes take our lives for granted and forget the beauty that they are. As we get lost in the worlds, we have created for ourselves. We manage our lives the best we can, but outside of God, the best we can muster is not very good. My business failed because I didn't understand the need to be adaptable. Are our lives stuck in neutral because we fail to recognize the need for being adaptable? Just like the work we put into our shows, and the magic of it when it all comes together, God is constantly working on our behalf to make this existence a beautiful experience for anyone who will allow it. Yet, if we are too comfortable in our own worlds and refuse to budge, this is why God makes the proverbial nest uncomfortable in order for us to see a need for change. The only time we truly do open our minds to change is when the change seems less stressful than staying the same. Whatever the case may be, God knows what it takes to get us jump-started in life again. God is not the god a lot of us would imagine he is. God is only a patient father waiting for his children to come to the understanding that we can't do life without the Creator of it.

May God richly bless you and yours.

Chapter 9

K.I.S.S. SYSTEM

What a name for a chapter of a book, huh? For those of us who don't know or who need a reminder, K.I.S.S. means, "Keep It Stupidly Simple." For those of us who like it a little more blunt, it's "Keep It Simple, Stupid." Either way, it's a wonderful life philosophy that many of us could benefit from if we just exercised it. Trust me, it's not hard to master; it is, however, hard to start. Just like when we need that nudge to get off our lazy butts and go to the gym to exercise, we need the same kind of nudge to make the choice to keep things simple.

We want to have authority and power over everything that happens in our lives. If something is beneficial, we accept it, and if it seems harmful, we reject it. The problem? Life doesn't usually come to us that way. Often, we don't have a choice in what happens; life just happens the way it happens. Good, bad, or indifferent, life doesn't ask us permission to be the way it is. It is (say it with me) the way it is. Other than saying no, that's the single most powerful phrase we can learn: "It is what it is."

Things are the way they are. Life usually turns out the way it has by the choices we've made. Every action we make has a reaction, and we can most certainly control the actions we make. However, the issue is that this pertains to us all. We live in a huge world with billions of people, with lots of varying views and opinions, and we all are constantly making different choices.

What may seem right to one may be totally wrong to the other. So, there are many, many actions with reactions being made every single second of every single moment of our existence, by everyone living in our world. I can control my choices, but I have no control or authority over anyone else's. This is where it gets interesting. Like a wave traveling across the ocean, the more actions and reactions that are being made, the more waves are being created and sent in any and every direction. Eventually, all these waves will meet. Where or when is anyone's guess, but eventually they will meet at the same place and the same time.

In leading my life, I have developed my own opinions and lived by a moral standard I have determined to be right. So have you. So has everyone. When we were growing up, we weren't smart enough to realize how big this world really is. We knew what we knew in our little world, and that was pretty much it. Bluntly, our world was all about us. We all went through that stage of life. But this becomes a problem when we've become stunted in our growth and we still see the world that way when we should have matured past that. It's long past time to come to the realization that this is a big earth with a huge variety of people and opinions.

God is endlessly creative, so we should expect variations of pretty much everything. There will be differences, there will be other opinions than our own, there will be alternate points of view. When our wave of action and reaction crosses paths with others, it may very well generate the exact opposite actions and reactions. This is where God's creativity becomes real to us, and what should be celebrated is far too often feared and rejected. We close our minds because it goes against what we have determined to be beneficial. We label it harmful, and we automatically reject it. My beliefs work for me, so there's no room left for yours. Yet if we took time to learn from one another and explore the why behind the what, we could become more mature and have a more fulfilled existence. Why? Because the more we see how creative and beautifully made we each are, we start to realize we're all the same. The only difference is the way we approach life and how we manage it. The more we can accept one another and our differences, the more we grow as human beings. Perhaps by seeing how someone else handles something differently than we do, we may very well learn something new, and it might even be a better way than our own.

For whatever reason I always felt as though I had to eat the whole bagel, which sometimes was not enough, and depending on my appetite that day, sometimes too much. I was about forty-one when I first realized I didn't have to eat the whole bagel. I was at a little ma-and-pa restaurant, and I noticed they had halved the bagels and served one half while putting the other back in the bag. What a wonderful idea, I thought. That's the solution to my problem. I can just do that too. I would cook the whole bagel regardless if I felt like eating it all or not. It took me all those years to realize what I thought was the best way, was just me being closed minded and not open to alternatives. I did things my way, and that was what worked for me, until I was introduced to another, better way. Too many of us fall into the same category of being stuck in what works for us, without being receptive to the notion there may be another way. We've found what works for us and we're off and running. There is an epidemic right under our noses and we don't want to acknowledge it, because too many of us choose that way to cope with life and its struggles.

Drugs, drugs, and more drugs. That seems to be the flavor of the week in today's society. Yet, instead of a fad that goes away as quickly as it comes around, this fad is growing alarmingly worse, and doesn't seem to be going away anytime soon. As long as there is a demand for something, people will find a way to supply it. Our hunger for pharmaceutical drugs has grown to epidemic levels. This is a huge problem that, left unchecked, will destroy us. I get it—I've been there, done that. It makes life so much easier when we have that little edge to help us get through the day, but we're looking in the wrong place for the wrong edge.

God has given us a remedy to whatever we may be sick from, all the way from eating honey for a bad stomach to learning how to give and receive forgiveness for spiritual health. Everything pertaining to our human condition had been dealt with in the Bible, God's Word. That's right, the Bible is the written Word of what God, our Creator, has said. We say that all the time, but do we really make the connection? This is what God says.

All we have to do is look up what we want to know in the Bible. Giving and receiving forgiveness (1 John 1:7-10), need comfort (Isaiah 41:10), need encouragement (Psalms 9:9-10), God has already replied to our prayer, and it's written in the Bible. But we have found it easier to take mind-altering substances instead of just reading the solution to what our Creator has already said about every issue we face. This is just being lazy. God has given us solutions to every issue we face; it's up to us to learn and practice them. It takes effort, and to some degree a certain level of discomfort, but it's the only way to learn how to live life and live it together with everyone who's going through the same thing we are.

We have two choices in life. There is a right way and a wrong way to live it. Jesus said the road to destruction is wide and easy and the road to salvation is narrow and hard (Matthew 7:13–14). Is he right on, or what? It's easy to take a drug because we've never learned how to deal with our anxiety, depression, or whatever ails our mental health. These problems and many more mental issues are very real. We all deal with them; it's how we deal with them that makes the difference. Do we go the wide and easy way and just go to the doctor to get a drug that makes us forget the problem until it's time to take more drugs? Or do we roll up our sleeves and go the hard and narrow way, putting in the time and effort to finding out the why behind the way our mental state has become? We have choices. We don't call it growing pains because it's easy. Growing and maturing, especially the older we get, is hard. It takes time and effort. We can learn how life is done right, in harmony with our Creator, or we can continue doing it wrong and half-assed until our time eventually runs out. The choice is ours.

The more attention we put into managing our lives, the better we become at it. Practice makes perfect, right? You bet. Our mental state should be a priority and not an afterthought. Whatever our mental state is, it will eventually find its way to the surface and come shining through into our physical state. So, instead of constantly putting on a show for all to see, why not figure out what needs to be done so we can be comfortable in our own mental state? It all starts by accepting the fact that we are not God. No matter how hard we try, the only person we have control over is ourselves. We can only try to persuade others to see life as we do; we can't make the choice for them. When all the different choices being made converge in one area and one point in time, we need to start by opening our mind, and become accepting. I'm not saying we have to accept everything and everyone's point of view; rather, we have to be mindful and respectful that it's their choice how they choose to live.

Life gets so chaotic and confusing at times because we're taking on more than we should. We continuously contemplate scenarios from the information we've gathered and come up with so many different outcomes, it's a wonder we have any time for anything else. We turn over in our mind every possible way we can rationally think of to whatever issue we may be facing, trying to be our own god. We want to keep that control over our lives, and we do what we must in order to have life work out the way we think it should for our own benefit. That's why we try so hard to figure out what's going to happen and prepare ourselves for whatever outcome we could possibly think of that could happen.

If we would only learn how to let life be what it is and quit trying to guess and somehow determine its outcome, we would be so much happier and would have such a better state of mental health. People are anxious because they feel as though they can't manage life anymore, and they're right. They've become so worn out over trying to keep life in an order they find acceptable and not accepting it for what it is that their mental state has fallen to an unhealthy level. Medications may be the answer for a time, but not for the duration. We all need help from time to time, and if we need help from medication that's fine, but it's not the final solution.

God is offering us a worry-free existence, when or if we accept it (Matthew 6:25-34). God blessed a man through me the other day at the grocery store, where he had me give the guy 100 dollars towards his groceries. I've been doing stuff like that every time God prompts me to, which is pretty much every time I go somewhere. Just be a blessing. I've gotten a lot of reactions when I do this, but this one particular reaction sort of caught me off guard. The guy who I gave the money to actually seemed to take offense to it. He literally got mad. I shot back and told the guy if he didn't want it, to give it to someone else, but I've done what God asked me to, so do what you want.

Why can't we just be content with being blessed, and take it for what it is, a blessing? This is what God does, he is constantly blessing us, and we don't even perceive it. We don't get it because we don't know God as good as we think we do. When we get ourselves out of the way, and operate in the system God intended for us in the beginning, we will begin to recognize the constant blessing our God is. The man God blessed through me got mad because he's slow to comprehend love. His first reaction is probably taking offense to me, because maybe he thought I was pointing out his weakness by insinuating he needed the money. Not at all.

God doesn't point out our weakness to hurt us in any way. God does however supply our needs, and is ready and willing to do it every time they may arise. How he does it is anyone's guess, but the more faith we put in him to do it, the more he will show us he will. God has offered us all to be adopted in his vast family, but there's only room for one God, and we are not the one.

We are the only one who can fight our battles, and the more training we have, the more effective we will be. We may have allies, but in the end, the war is won or lost by the choices we have made in our respective battles. This life is all about learning and growing, maturing in all areas of our being. Our mental health is a vital part of our being, yet it is far too often ignored. This life is a marathon, and it will take time and effort to do it at its most effective levels. None of us are masters, and we're all learning as we go.

When someone's wave meets our wave and the sea gets choppy and unstable, let's accept it for what it is. Life may go sideways, and there's no controlling it. The only control we do have is how we process the information. Do we accept life is the way it is at this moment? Do we lose sleep over running every possible outcome over and over in our minds? Do we come up with our own scenarios and try to manipulate the situation so that it will work out to our liking? Well, only one of those solutions will keep our mental state healthy. It is what it is.

We need to learn life through experience, but if we're our own teacher, there's nothing being learned; we're only living according to what we think is acceptable, and that could be very wrong and uninformed. I can look in my backyard and see five different species of trees; they're all different, but in another way, they are all the same. They may look different and grow different, but they all take our used oxygen and turn it back to useful air. We, too, are exactly the same, every single one of us. Just like the trees, we only look different and grow different, but in the end, we all have the same function. So, let's learn how to grow together, and accept life for what it is, not how we would individually like it. It's all about us, not just me or just you.

When we accept God as our God, and give him the rightful place he deserves in our lives, he takes away the burden of life and living that we have placed upon ourselves with the system we have developed through our limited understanding. Our system says we provide for ourselves; God's system says he will provide. This is how we apply the K.I.S.S. system. God will provide anything and everything, but what we sometimes get caught up on is how he does it. Sometimes he will just provide the way to get it, and we have to go get it. Sometimes he will just give it to us, like he did with the man he gave 100 dollars to through me. However he does it, we need to understand he will do it.

So, in learning how to apply the K.I.S.S. system, we just accept life for what it is. God gave me 100 dollars, thank you very much. That's it. No need to rationalize why or the motives behind it, just accept it, and be thankful. I gave the guy 100 dollars and told him why, to put towards his groceries. When the next need comes up, God will provide the remedy for that as well, but until the next need arises, enjoy the blessing of our God.

This K.I.S.S. system is universal. I use it in just about every situation in which I find myself. It pays off in the long run when I just accept things the way they are presented and don't waste a single ounce of energy on trying to figure out why. Instead, I choose to use my energy on how I cope with it. I can't control the ocean, so I'll make sure my boat is strong and not taking water, and I'll just ride the waves till I get to calmer seas.

It never dawned on me till recently how little we have to do in the management of our lives. The more I study, the more I see how everything that is necessary and vital to our functioning is taken care of. Even our bodies have an autopilot. When all is working properly, our bodies function with or without our consent. Our bodies supply their own air, and they breathe on their own. Our hearts pump the needed blood all by themselves. Our bodies are a self-sustaining work of art. The only thing our body needs from us is to supply it with the fuel it needs to operate, and even that has been provided by the earth we live on. Everything has been put in order and made readily available to supply us with what we need in order to function as humans.

If we break it all down, we see everything is already taken care of. And I mean everything. Nothing has been left to chance. Everything that pertains to us and our existence as human beings has been taken care of by our Creator, God. All that has been left up to us is how we manage our lives. God has given us a powerful supercomputer in our brains, and these in turn give us the power needed to be a responsible manager of our respective lives. Our minds are a powerful thing. From the day we were born, our brains have gathered, stored, and processed all kinds of information. Over time, we become aware of our existence. We start to understand that we are alive and what it means to be alive. This is the one thing that our Creator has given us power over. Everything else takes care of itself, except our minds. God has given us the power to manage how we experience our existence, and with that power comes responsibility. The first thing we would be wise to learn is the single most powerful thing about having power, which is knowing when and when not to use it. Just because we have power over something doesn't necessarily mean we have to constantly exercise it. I'm in no way implying we should not use our brains; I'm saying it's okay and to some extent necessary to not overthink certain things.

May God richly bless you and yours.

Chapter 10

FINALLY

I pray you enjoyed reading this as much as I did writing it. Yet if there's one thing I wish we would all take away from this and any other literature about our spirituality, it's this:

> So, do not fear, for I am with you; do not be dismayed, for I am your God. I will strengthen you and help you; I will uphold you with my righteous right hand.
>
> For I am the Lord, your God, who takes hold of your right hand and says to you, Do not fear; I will help you. (Isaiah 41:10 & 13 KJV)

This is by far one of the most beautiful verses of the Bible, given to us by our Creator. Also, please consider that a lot of God's promises are contingent on which way we choose to live, meaning God will do this when we do that. These verses have no conditions attached, this is who our God is, and it's what he does. This love is available to any and all.

The foundation of all God's promises is belief. That's it, just believe. How beautiful is that? Our Creator will do anything and everything for us if we just think he can and will. Belief seems like an easy ticket to cash in, but we all seem to have such a hard time with it. We may feel inadequate. How could a loving God want anything to do with such a bad sinner like me? We may feel as though we owe God something for everything he's done for us, and work extra hard at trying to repay or earn his love. There are many reasons why we have a hard time with belief, but I assure you, with practice, patience, and perseverance, we will get better at it, and it won't be something we do. It will be who we are.

Throughout this book, we've explored some of the attributes of God, and his steadfast love towards us. We've touched on how God works, and some of the why behind what he does. We've discussed how important our overall health is, not only to us, but our God as well. Friends, it is my hope we shed some light on some of the deeper questions we have about this life and living, and we've allowed ourselves to stay true to the process. In the end, that's all this is: a growth and maturation process as God takes us from babies to well-matured adults. There are many things we don't know, and God will certainly lead us into situations where we have no clue, and our only avenue is to totally rely on him, and it's scary.

"Do not be afraid" or some form of that phrase is in the Bible more than 145 times. If something is that important to be mentioned over and over, there may be some merit to it. God knows who we are, and we need to be taught who he is, and God uses real life situations, with real life people, in the real world. When we are being taught by God, most of his lessons are new to us, and we don't have any reference for it, that's what makes it scary and if we're not careful we'll allow the fear to engulf us and ruin our progress. It always seems as though we're in the dark with God, and it seems that way because we are. God is constantly teaching us who he is by bringing us to situations beyond our control, so he can show us firsthand his love for us as he cares for us, provides for us, heals us, and resurrects us. All done right in front of our eyes, meant to strengthen and grow our belief.

God is a great father. We are the only thing hindering our lives from being full of joy, happiness, and excitement. We will not find life anywhere else outside of God. God knows what he's trying to accomplish when he has us wherever he has us, doing whatever he has us doing. My education will be tailored just for me, yours will be suited just for you, but one thing that's consistent is God's love for us. God will not allow anything to harm us. No matter what situation you may find yourself in, God has a reason for allowing it. It becomes our job, and let me stress, our *only* job, to allow God his lordship over our lives as we work our way through his process, and slowly begin to understand what we're being taught.

There's an order and design to our universe. Nothing just happens. Everything happens the way it should. There is a lot going on around us that we have no clue about and that doesn't pertain to us. When we learn how to manage our powerful minds, we can defend against letting in the nonsense and accept what's beneficial to our individual lives. We won't have to accept and analyze every bit of information; if it's important, God will let us know. The world is going to be the world, with all the nonsense that's included in it. We can grow in our belief in Jesus and learn from him, or we can continue to try to control our own destiny and get frustrated when we see it never works the way we would like it to.

Let's give our minds a rest and stop thinking everything through and through. Let God do his work in us and accept it for what it is. I guarantee to anyone who reads this that God is trustworthy, and whatever he's doing is for our benefit, even when it may seem like he's lost his mind and our world is spinning out of control. God wants us all in heaven with him, and he has made it so simple for us to accomplish that. The only reason we may find ourselves not in heaven is by our own choice. We need to quit allowing our enemy any advantage and start guarding our minds. The more we learn to trust Jesus, the easier life becomes, because we see the simplicity and honesty of our Creator.

Even as I write this, I am trusting Jesus like I never have before, and I'm seeing life as I've never seen it before. If someone had told me this is where I'd be, doing what I'm doing at this point in my life, I would have belly laughed right in their face. I couldn't have imagined this in my wildest dreams on my best day, much less would I have had the design to set it all up like it is. My point is that there is no doubt in my mind that we can trust God. I know that we can, because I have and am. I hope anyone who reads this will allow God to prove that Jesus is telling us the truth in everything he says and does. It takes time and experience to hear his words and learn his lessons. Don't try to outthink God; it won't happen. We can't out-create the original Creator. Let's learn to accept life on its terms and conditions and so expand on our trust from experience to experience as we do life with Jesus as our guide.

Be patient with our God. He knows what he's doing, and in time it will make perfect sense, and you will see why we were taught the way we were. Friends, it is my belief that we are not only being taught how to live life in the here and now, while we are in the restraints of time. But this is what life will look like when we reach our eternal destination. God will be our God, and we will be his people. In heaven we will want for nothing, everything will be provided, and we will live an existence of perfect harmony between ourselves and our Creator.

We are the creation, and we need to be taught everything, from who we are to who our Creator is. God is offering us this education, but it is through him, from him, by him. Meaning, we have to learn how to forget our limited understanding of what we think we know, and allow ourselves to be taught what we need to know. As we touched on, God uses real situations, in our real lives, to teach us the truth of life. We need to learn to focus our entire attention on God. When our attention is on God, and our priority is him, we can learn how to use the tools he has given us. If we don't have God as our focus, we will far too often resort back to our limited knowledge.

There's so much we need to learn, and we need to be mindful that we're consistently being taught. The Bible says put God first in everything and all else will fall into place (Proverbs 3:6). When we are constantly mindful of God, and understand we're consistently being taught, we live our lives accordingly. The next time someone gets in our face upset about lord knows what, instead of us resorting to our known behavior, and firing right back with our own set of "insights" about the situation, we'll understand that this is an opportunity to use the tools of understanding that God has given us. The next time we're wronged, and we have the right to even the score, we'll be mindful of God and use the tool of forgiveness he has given us.

In this book, we have discussed numerous traits of God, and have offered various thoughts and ideas designed to help us keep an open mind and heart towards our God as he brings us from seed to strong, well rooted oaks. God will always work with us in whatever area we may lack, and that is solely at his discretion. You and I being the creation have no clue where we may lack, this is why we have to keep an open heart and mind as God gives us new perspectives about what we've learned about life and living. Just like me with my bagels always thinking I had to eat the whole thing at once. I never would have changed my behavior if I had never been shown a better way. God in his word (Bible) has given us the necessary tools on how to live a quality life, once we agree with him that we need to be taught, God will bring us to real life situations in order for us to use those tools, and practice as often and as long as it takes until it becomes who we are and what we do.

I pray this literature helps us in whatever capacity it does. We've touched on numerous subjects, but the main thing I would hope we take away from reading this is the importance of keeping an open mind. God is the original Creator and creates worlds and the life in them out of nothing at all. God will do things that will blow our literal minds and leave us in awe as we witness it. This is why an open mind is critical to our success. Don't discount God and his power. Just because God has chosen to not use his power in multiple areas concerning us, does not mean he doesn't have it. Kindness is not weakness, it's strength. Allow God to teach us who we are, who he is, and any other thing God would have us to know about.

You are a one-of-a-kind priceless work of art, and God has placed so much of his beauty and wisdom inside of you. Yet, it takes God to draw out what he created in you. Please allow it. Stay faithful to the process. It takes what it takes, and it will not be comfortable. But in the end, God will stay faithful to you even if we don't stay faithful to him. God wants us to experience life as it was created to be, and not only in the here and now, but for eternity. Practice staying faithful to the process, and you won't be disappointed. No matter where you find yourself in this world, know God has planted you there, and is tenderly taking care of you every second of every day. Keep God first in your thoughts and focus your attention on him as he brings us from death to life to living life as it was intended.

May God richly bless you and yours.

www.ingramcontent.com/pod-product-compliance
Lightning Source LLC
LaVergne TN
LVHW011726060526
838200LV00051B/3046